OSP: An Environment for Operating System Projects

Michael Kifer • Scott A. Smolka

SUNY at Stony Brook

ADDISON-WESLEY PUBLISHING COMPANY
Reading, Massachusetts • Menlo Park, California • New York
Don Mills, Ontario • Wokingham, England • Amsterdam
Bonn • Sydney • Singapore • Tokyo • Madrid • San Juan

Reproduced by Addison-Wesley from camera-ready copy supplied by the authors.

ISBN 0-201-54887-9

8 9 10-CRS-97 96

PREFACE

Welcome to *OSP*, an Operating System Project. *OSP* is a collection of modules that together implement a modern-day operating system. Each module performs a basic operating system service such as device scheduling, cpu scheduling, interrupt handling, file management, memory management, process management, resource management, and interprocess communication.

OSP is a simulated system—there is a special module, called *SIMCORE*, that provides the illusion of a computer system with a dynamically evolving collection of user processes to be multi-programmed. All the other modules of *OSP* are built to respond appropriately to the simulator-generated events that drive the operating system.

Over the course of the semester, you will be given several assignments, each of which normally consists of implementing one of the *OSP* modules.[1] You will also be given instructions on how to compile and link your module with the rest of *OSP*. The end result will be a new and complete operating system, which you can now run in the simulated environment provided by *SIMCORE*.

SIMCORE offers a number of different ways in which you can interact with *OSP* during simulation. When simulation commences, you will be prompted for the *simulation parameters*. *SIMCORE* uses these parameters to decide whether the system should be I/O-bound or cpu-bound, how often to generate requests for various system resources, how long the simulation should last, etc.

At any point during simulation, you can request a *snapshot*: *SIMCORE* will display various tables that convey the current state of

---

[1] Sometimes you will be asked to implement some support modules as well; for example, the device interrupt handler when implementing the device scheduler.

the system, e.g., the state of memory, device queues, event queues, the ready queue, open file tables, and more. You can also change the simulation parameters during a snapshot break. By systematically modifying the simulation parameters, you can test your system under a wide variety of conditions. This enables you to reach a high level of confidence in the correctness of your *OSP* implementation, and to evaluate its performance characteristics. *SIMCORE* also has a *trace facility* for tracking the occurrences of individual events, such as process creation, requests to read a file, requests to send messages, and device interrupts.

In order to prevent corruption of the system state, *SIMCORE* monitors all events in the system, keeping its own copy of the system state. Whenever it detects an unanticipated and fatal error in the behavior of a module, execution is terminated, and an informative error message is printed. If *SIMCORE* deems the error to be non-fatal, it issues a warning and continues. Between the snapshot breaks, trace facility, and diagnostic capabilities, *SIMCORE* offers you an extensive environment in which to monitor and debug your programs.

This book is organized as follows. Chapter 1 constitutes the *OSP* programmer's manual and reference guide. Section 1.2 presents the overall architecture of *OSP*, and the *OSP* modules are described in detail in the remaining sections. Included in each of the latter sections is a brief discussion of the general concepts of operating system design as they relate to the module in question. Each of these sections also defines the procedures that are imported and exported by the module.

Chapter 2 is a user's guide that explains how to compile and run your programs, the meaning of the statistics and error messages generated by *OSP*, and how to submit your assignments. For ease of reference, a glossary of *OSP* data structures and data types is also included.

To get the big picture of *OSP*, we suggest that you first read Chapter 2 and then Sections 1.1 to 1.4 of Chapter 1. The remaining sections of Chapter 1 should be dipped into when a particular module has been assigned as a project, or when you simply would like to understand a module in greater detail.

OSP was developed at SUNY, Stony Brook, and borrowed several important ideas from an earlier project headed by Art Bernstein. We would like to gratefully acknowledge the contributions of Kit Lo, Nathan Tam, and Andrew Moncrieffe who implemented the first version of *OSP*. Subsequent enhancements are due to Jusuf Anwar, Lawrence Kwok, and Sankar Raman. Many people have used preliminary versions of $\mathcal{OSP}$ in their classes and have given us valuable feedback. In particular, we would like to thank Amr El Abbadi, Michael Fischer, Larry Hall, Bruce Parker, Mark Roth, and Gene Stark.

CONTENTS

1

PROGRAMMING *OSP*

This chapter is organized as follows. We first discuss the modular interface of *OSP*, and suggest guidelines to be followed when faced with an *OSP* programming assignment. This is followed by a brief account of the functionality of the *OSP* modules and their interconnection. We then present the architecture of the underlying simulated machine and the data structures used to represent it.

The main body of Chapter 1 contains a detailed description of all of the *OSP* modules. This description includes, for each module $\mathcal{M}$, two *interface tables*: one specifies the calling sequences of the routines *internal* to module $\mathcal{M}$ that may be used by other modules; and the other specifies the calling sequences of the *external* routines that belong to other modules but are used by $\mathcal{M}$.

To obtain a general knowledge of the internals of *OSP*, it is advised to first read Sections 1.1 through 1.4. Other sections need be read only when specific modules have been assigned as a project. Occasionally, it will be necessary to consult the glossary to find definitions of data types referred to in one module, but defined in another.

OSP is written in the C programming language. As such, the definitions of all data types and procedure definitions are given in C.

1.1 Getting Started

OSP is a collection of modules that together implement a modern-day operating system. Several times during the semester, you will be given an assignment in which you are to implement one or more of the *OSP* modules. You will also be given instructions on how to compile and link your modules with the rest of the *OSP* system (see also Chapter 2). The end result will be a new and complete operating system, which you can run in the simulated environment provided by the *SIMCORE* module of *OSP*.

When a module $\mathcal{M}$ is assigned as a project, your job is to supply the code for the internal routines of $\mathcal{M}$. This code should rely on the external routines to perform various functions delegated to other modules. In the course of implementing $\mathcal{M}$, you may find it helpful to write some additional routines to carry out auxiliary tasks. Since these routines do not appear in the table of internal routines, they cannot be called by other modules.

To clarify, let us consider a specific example. Suppose you have been asked to implement module *CPU* (cpu scheduling). After having read the Preface, Sections 1.1 through 1.4, and Chapter 2, the first thing to do is turn to Section 1.7. Here you will find a detailed description of *CPU*, as well as the tables of internal and external routines for this module.

CPU has three internal routines: *cpu_init*( ), *insert_ready*( ), and *dispatch*( ). Therefore, to implement this module you will have to supply the code for these routines, following the guidelines that appear in Section 1.7. These guidelines are not entirely self-contained, and you are therefore expected to know the material from the course text concerning cpu scheduling.

CPU has four external routines: *prepage*( ) and *start_cost*( ) of module *MEMORY* (memory management), and *set_timer*( ) and *get_clock*( ) of module *SIMCORE* (the simulator). These routines should be used to help you implement the cpu scheduler. For example, to prepage a process and to estimate the cost of the prepaging, you should make use of the routines *prepage*( ) and *start_cost*( ). Both of these routines are external to *CPU* but internal to *MEMORY*. Similarly, to set the time quantum for round-robin scheduling and to obtain the current simulated time, you should call the routines *set_timer*( ) and *get_clock*( ) of *SIMCORE*.

1.2 Architecture of *OSP*

OSP consists of ten primary modules whose interaction is depicted in Figure 1.1. In this diagram an arrow between modules, say from $\mathcal{M}$ to $\mathcal{N}$, means that routines in $\mathcal{M}$ may call routines in $\mathcal{N}$. The following table gives the names of the modules plus a short description of their functionality.

SIMCORE	core of the simulator
DIALOG	run-time interface to *OSP*
INTER	general interrupt handling
IOSVC	I/O monitor calls
DEVINT	device interrupts
PAGEINT	page fault interrupts
PROCSVC	process management monitor calls
TIMEINT	timer interrupts
MEMORY	memory management
CPU	cpu scheduling
DEVICES	device management
FILES	file organization
RESOURCES	resource management
SOCKETS	interprocess communication
PROTOCOLS	protocol support for the *SOCKETS* module

The architecture of the simulated computer consists of a cpu, two disks, a drum used as a swap area for virtual memory, a vectored interrupt facility, and virtual memory hardware.

1.2.1 CPU

Associated with the cpu are the following hardware components:

- interval timer
- clock
- interrupt vector
- page table base register

Module *SIMCORE* (Section 1.3) provides routines to set the interval timer and to read the contents of the clock. The page table base register

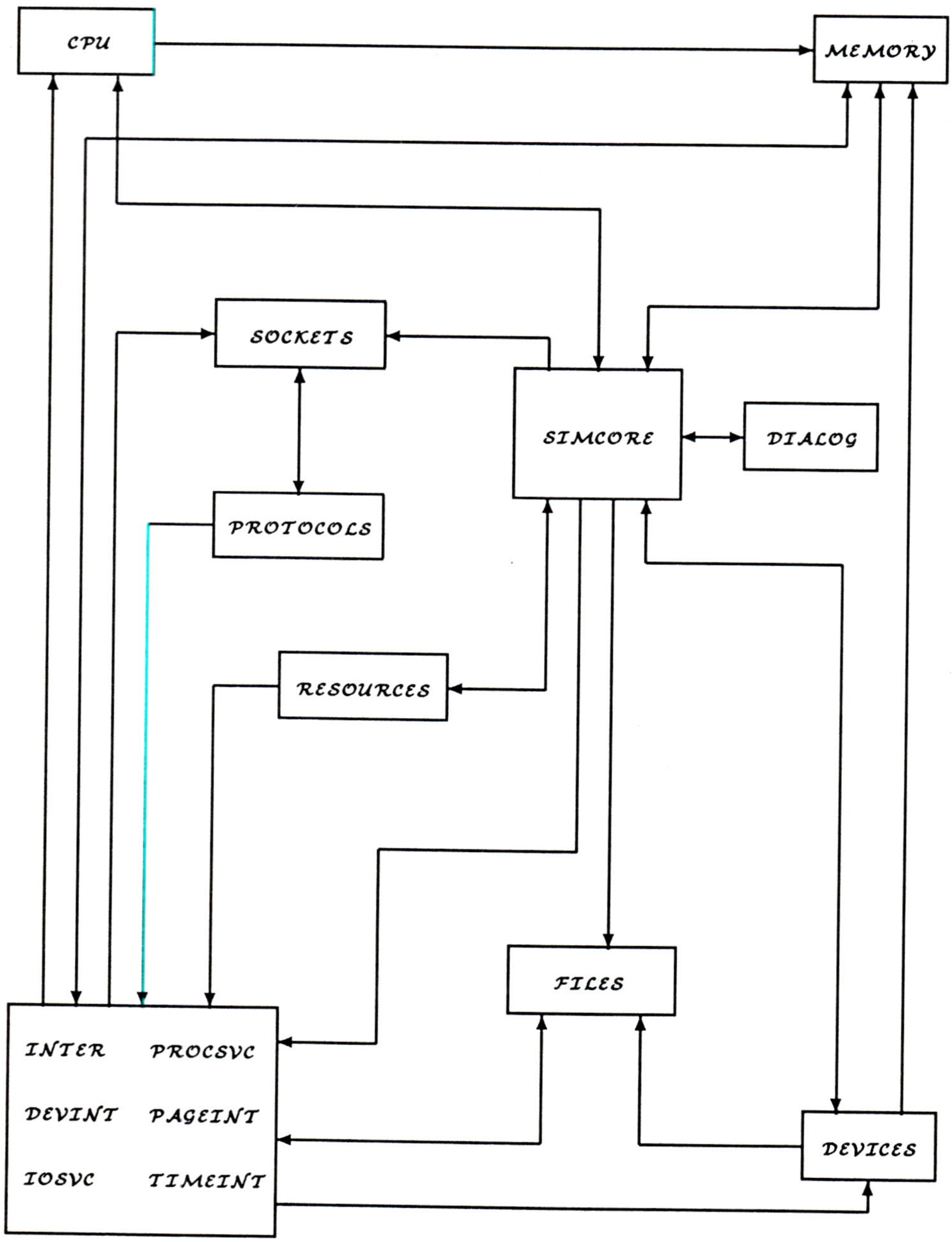

FIGURE 1.1 The Module Structure of *OSP*

and the interrupt vector are described below.

The simulated machine also consists of I/O devices in the form of two disks and a drum, which are used for user I/O and virtual memory management, respectively. Routines to initiate I/O on these devices are provided by *SIMCORE*. Disks are described in detail in Section 1.8 (module *DEVICES*), and the drum is discussed in Section 1.6 (module *MEMORY*).

1.2.2 Interrupt Vector

The type of *OSP* interrupts is defined as follows:

```
typedef enum {
     iosvc, devint, pagefault, startsvc, termsvc,
     killsvc, waitsvc, sigsvc, timeint
}           INT_TYPE;
```

Interrupt handling is discussed in Section 1.5. The simulated vectored interrupt facility has the following structure:

```
typedef struct int_vector_node INT_VECTOR;
struct int_vector_node    {
    INT_TYPE cause;   /* cause of the interrupt                   */
    PCB *pcb;         /* pcb to start/kill, if cause =            */
                      /* startsvc/killsvc; pcb that caused        */
                      /* page fault, if cause = pagefault         */
    int page_id;      /* page that caused page fault              */
    int dev_id;       /* device that caused devint                */
    EVENT *event;     /* event assoc'd with waitsvc/sigsvc        */
    IORB *iorb;       /* iorb assoc'd with iosvc call             */
};

INT_VECTOR Int_Vector; /* the interrupt vector                    */
```

1.2.3 Physical Memory

The simulated computer provides hardware support for paged virtual memory. In particular, memory is divided into fixed-size page frames (of size *PAGE_SIZE* bytes), a page table base register (*PTBR*) is provided, and the drum serves as a swap area for user processes. The data structures corresponding to physical memory now follow.

```
PAGE_TBL *PTBR;          /* page table base register         */
```

PAGE_TBL is the data type for page tables, and is defined in Section 1.6 (module *MEMORY*). *PTBR* is a cpu register used to locate the page table of the current process. Also, the field *PTBR→pcb* provides a convenient way to access the process control block (*pcb*) of that process.

```
typedef struct frame_node FRAME;
struct frame_node   {
    BOOL free;           /* true, if the frame is free       */
    PCB *pcb;            /* process that owns the frame      */
    int page_id;         /* virtual page id - index into     */
                         /* the page table pcb->page_tbl     */
    BOOL dirty;          /* true, if frame was modified      */
    int lock_count;      /* # of I/O locks on this frame     */
    int *hook;           /* user can hook anything here      */
};
FRAME Frame_Tbl[MAX_FRAME];
```

The last entry, *hook*, is part of many standard data types in *OSP*. It facilitates the "hook-up" of whatever additional information the user may want to incorporate in the standard structures, e.g., to add additional fields to these structures.

1.2.4 General Data Types

The following type definitions appear throughout this chapter.

```
typedef enum {
    false, true          /* the Boolean data type            */
}         BOOL;

typedef enum {
    fail, ok             /* OSP routines' exit codes         */
}         EXIT_CODE;

typedef enum {
    read, write          /* type of I/O requests             */
}         IO_ACTION;
```

```
typedef enum {
    load, store         /* type of memory references    */
}           REFER_ACTION;
```

1.3 The Simulator – Module *SIMCORE*

The events that drive the *OSP* modules are generated by a simulator implemented in *SIMCORE*. This module simulates the execution of user programs, which in turn are multi-programmed by the rest of *OSP*. In addition, *SIMCORE* simulates an interval timer and I/O devices. This is the only module of *OSP* that is not intended as a project for students. The particular types of events generated are:

- requests for process creation, termination, and abortion
- requests to synchronize processes on signals
- virtual memory references
- timer interrupts
- I/O requests
- device interrupts
- requests for resources
- requests to send and receive messages over sockets

SIMCORE uses a set of *simulation parameters* to decide how often to generate events of a given type, and to determine other aspects of the simulation environment; e.g., the length of the simulation, the cpu time quantum, etc. As described below, simulation parameters can be changed interactively by the user. A complete account of the simulation parameters is given in Chapter 2.

The simulator "charges" the various modules of *OSP* for cpu time, I/O activity, and other resources, so that it may accumulate statistics that can be used to estimate the performance of the modules written by the students. Statistics include: cpu time used, cpu utilization, system throughput, memory utilization, number of I/O operations performed on the various devices, and the number of page faults and page replacements.

In order to prevent corruption to the integrity of the system state, the simulator monitors all events in the system, keeping its own copy of the system state. In many cases, this enables *SIMCORE* to verify the correctness of the behavior of student modules. Whenever it detects an unanticipated and fatal error in the behavior of a module, execution is terminated and an informative error message is issued. If the simulator deems the error to be non-fatal, it issues a warning and continues. For example, a reference to virtual memory that should have caused a page fault but did not, will result in the simulator terminating, while not using the "dirty bit" optimization in memory management will result in a warning. In general, *SIMCORE* is able to recognize and report a wide variety of errors and inefficiencies in student programs.

Internal Routine	Called By

`siodev( iorb );`
`IORB *iorb;`
Performs the I/O operation specified in the iorb.
	DEVICES

`siodrum(action, pcb, page_id, frame_id);`
`IO_ACTION action;`
`PCB *pcb;`
`int page_id, frame_id;`
Transfers page between main memory and the drum; *action* is either *read* or *write*; with *read* the page *page_id* is brought from the drum into the frame *frame_id*; with *write* the contents of the frame *frame_id* is saved in the swap area for the process represented by *pcb*, in the block designated for the page *page_id*.
	MEMORY

`int get_clock();` Returns the current simulated time; may be used for implementing the "working set" memory management strategy, aging-based cpu scheduling policies, or to trigger deadlock detection.	*MEMORY*, *CPU*, *RESOURCES*

`set_timer( time_quantum );`
`int time_quantum;`
Resets the simulated timer.
	CPU, *TIMEINT*

The Debugging Interface to *SIMCORE*

SIMCORE lets the programmer view the system status (e.g., the state of memory and the devices, statistics) during simulation. A simulation parameter, called *snapshot_interval*, may be set by the user to indicate how often during simulation the system status is to be displayed. The user may also request a snapshot by hitting CTRL-Z. Each snapshot break also presents an opportunity for users to change the simulation parameters, and, as explained in module *DIALOG*, internal variables of their modules.

Internal Routine (*SIMCORE* debugging calls)	**Called By**
change_sim_params ( );	*DIALOG*
Changes simulation parameters at snapshot breaks. Prompts the user for the appropriate changes.	
print_sim_frame_tbl ( );	*DIALOG*
print_sim_dev_tbl ( );	*DIALOG*
print_sim_rsrc_tbl ( );	*DIALOG*
print_sim_socket_tbl ( );	*DIALOG*
print_sim_open_files_tbl ( );	*DIALOG*
print_sim_pcb_pool ( );	*DIALOG*
print_sim_disk_map ( );	*DIALOG*
print_sim_waiting_queue ( );	*DIALOG*
print_sim_prrb_queue ( );	*DIALOG*
These routines print the contents of the frame, device, resource, and socket tables, as well as the status of all active pcb records, disks, and queues. The importance of these routines is that they display the status of these data structures as they *should be* according to the simulator.	

After each snapshot is taken, or after a warning or an error message is issued, *SIMCORE* calls the routines *at_snapshot*( ), *at_warning*( ), and *at_error*( ) of *DIALOG*, respectively. The programmer can customize these "*at*"-routines to view the state of system tables or change simulation parameters by calling the routines provided by the debugging interface to *SIMCORE* .

Another important debugging feature of *OSP* is its *trace facility.* The student can direct the simulator to produce a list of all events (relevant to the specific assignment) that occurred during a simulation run. In case of an error, examining the trace of events may help locate the cause of the error. Many *OSP* data structures contain an id field. The value of this field is usually set by *SIMCORE* so that instances of a data structure can be easily identified within a trace. For other data structures, the id field can be set by the programmer as an optional debugging aid. In either case, it will be stated as a comment in the definition of a data structure whose responsibility it is to set the id field.

External Routine	Host Module
extern at_snapshot ( ); Called after a snapshot is taken; allows the programmer to alter simulation parameters and program variables.	*DIALOG*
extern at_warning ( );	*DIALOG*
extern at_error ( ); These routines are called right after a warning or an error message is printed by *SIMCORE*; students can use these routines to display internal variables of their programs exactly as they are at the moment when *SIMCORE* discovers an error. One can also use the routines in the debugging interface to *SIMCORE* to display the system status.	*DIALOG*

1.4 Run-time Interface and Debugging – Module *DIALOG*

This module provides three routines: *at_snapshot*( ), which is called by the simulator after each snapshot is taken or when the user hits CTRL-Z on the keyboard; *at_warning*( ), which is called right after a warning is issued; and *at_error*( ), which is called when an error is detected.

The contents of these routines depends on how the student intends to use the dialogue facility of *OSP*. If the student wants just to see the system status, then *at_snapshot*( ) need only issue a prompt about continuing the simulation. If, on the other hand, the student wants to change simulation parameters, such as *snapshot_interval*, *trace_switch*, or the job-stream intensity, which are local variables of *SIMCORE*, *at_snapshot*( ) must call *change_sim_params*( ) of *SIMCORE*. This routine prompts the user for the parameters to be changed and then performs the changes. Note that the *at_snapshot*( ) routine supplied with the standard *DIALOG* module does call *change_sim_params*( ).

Like *at_snapshot*( ), the routines *at_warning*( ) and *at_error*( ) can be used to display the status of the system by calling *print_sim_frame_tbl*( ), *print_sim_dev_tbl*( ), and other routines that constitute the debugging interface to *SIMCORE*. The status of variables local to the modules implemented by the student can also be displayed here. This is useful as it shows the status of these variables right at the moment when *SIMCORE* detects an error or issues a warning.

Dynamically changing the values of variables local to *OSP* modules implemented by students is also possible. Consider such a student module $\mathcal{M}$. The programmer should write a routine, say *tune_*$\mathcal{M}$( ), incorporate it into $\mathcal{M}$, and then call it from *at_snapshot*( ). This routine, being local to $\mathcal{M}$, will be able to change the value of any variable inside $\mathcal{M}$. Care should be exercised when writing the routines *tune_*$\mathcal{M}$( ) to ensure that they have no undesirable side effects. The same technique can be used to change the values of variables local to $\mathcal{M}$ from inside the routines *at_warning*( ) and *at_error*( ). The interface to *DIALOG* is given next:

Internal Routine	Called By
at_snapshot ( ); Provides a run-time interface to *OSP*; allows the user to change simulation parameters and program variables for debugging purposes.	*SIMCORE*
at_warning ( );	*SIMCORE*
at_error ( ); Like *at_snapshot*( ), but invoked at the time a warning or an error message is printed.	*SIMCORE*

External Routine	Host Module
extern change_sim_params ( ); Changes simulation parameters during snapshot breaks.	*SIMCORE*

External Routine (continued)	**Host Module**
extern print_sim_frame_tbl ( );	*SIMCORE*
extern print_sim_dev_tbl ( );	*SIMCORE*
extern print_sim_rsrc_tbl ( );	*SIMCORE*
extern print_sim_sockets_tbl ( );	*SIMCORE*
extern print_sim_open_files_tbl ( );	*SIMCORE*
extern print_sim_pcb_pool ( );	*SIMCORE*
extern print_sim_disk_map ( );	*SIMCORE*
extern print_sim_waiting_queue ( );	*SIMCORE*
extern print_sim_prrb_queue ( );	*SIMCORE*
These routines print the contents of the frame, device, resource, and socket tables, as well as the status of all active pcb records, disks, and queues; the importance of these routines is that they show the status of these data structures as they *should be* according to the simulator.	

1.5 Interrupt Handling – Module *INTER*

An interrupt is an event, such as the completion of an I/O operation or a monitor call, that causes the computer to stop normal processing and execute an instruction specifically reserved for the occasion. Normally, this instruction directs the cpu towards a kernel routine that interprets the interrupt and performs certain operations in response. In the process of generating an interrupt, the hardware records the cause of the interrupt and the address of the appropriate kernel routine in a reserved memory location called the *interrupt vector.* In *OSP*, interrupts can be of the following types:

Hardware interrupts:

- timer interrupt: *timeint*
- page fault: *pagefault*
- device interrupt: *devint*

Monitor calls:

- I/O (read, write): *iosvc*
- process control
  - start: *startsvc*
  - kill: *killsvc*
  - terminate: *termsvc*
  - signal: *sigsvc*
  - wait: *waitsvc*

Interrupts are supported in the simulated machine by means of the interrupt vector data structure *Int_Vector* (p. 5). An interrupt is generated, usually by the simulator but also by routines such as *refer*( ), *acquire*( ) or *release*( ), by calling procedure *gen_int_handler*( ) of this module; the cause of the interrupt is passed along in the interrupt vector. The general interrupt handler then calls a special-purpose handler, based on the cause of the interrupt. In an actual computer system, the act of invoking *gen_int_handler*( ) and recording the cause of the interrupt in *Int_Vector* is done in hardware. In $\mathcal{OSP}$, since the computer itself is simulated by $\mathcal{SIMCORE}$, it is the responsibility of the programmer to set up *Int_Vector* and call *gen_int_handler*( ) when an interrupt is to be simulated.

If a process was running at the time of an interrupt, its pcb can be found in *PTBR→pcb*. If no process was running at that time, then either *PTBR* = NULL, or *PTBR→pcb→status* ≠ *running*. Usually, *PTBR→pcb* is also the pcb of the process that caused the interrupt, with the notable exceptions *startsvc*, *killsvc*, and *pagefault*.

For interrupts of type *startsvc*, *killsvc*, and *pagefault*, which necessitate storing a pcb in the interrupt vector, the stored pcb (*Int_Vector.pcb*) typically is not the one of the process that issued the monitor call. For example, in the case of a *startsvc* interrupt, the process to be started (inserted into the ready queue) is a newly created process that has never run before. In the case of a *killsvc*, the process to be killed might be not the one that is currently running but one of the processes involved in a deadlock. The same is often true about page fault interrupts, which may be caused by I/O devices trying to lock main memory pages, rather than due to normal memory-referencing by running processes.

Interrupt processing represents a golden opportunity to take care of cpu scheduling concerns (see also module *CPU*, Section 1.7). In particular, when *gen_int_handler*( ) is entered, one should compute the just-completed cpu burst of the interrupted process, and update the accumulated cpu time of this process. (The cpu burst is obtained by subtracting the current contents of the clock from the *last_dispatch* field of the pcb.) Additionally, just before exiting *gen_int_handler*( ), routine *dispatch*( ) of *CPU* should be called to reschedule the ready processes.

Since the cpu scheduler may be called as part of interrupt processing, the running process before and after the interrupt may be different. The programmer should save the pcb of the process running before the interrupt, if it is needed for later use.

One word of caution about cpu scheduling. Because of the simulated nature of *OSP*, an interrupt may take place while another interrupt is being processed, i.e., interrupts may become nested. To keep track of nested interrupts, *gen_int_handler*( ) should maintain a static variable, say *interrupt_nest_level*, with initial value 0. Each time *gen_int_handler*( ) is entered, this variable must be incremented by 1; it must be decremented by 1 just before leaving the routine. Since, as explained below, a new process cannot be scheduled inside a nested call to *gen_int_handler*( ), updates to *accumulated_cpu* and *last_cpuburst* should be made only when *interrupt_nest_level* = 1, i.e., in the outermost invocation of *gen_int_handler*( ).

Similarly, the call to *dispatch*( ) should be made just before leaving the outermost invocation of *gen_int_handler*( ). *SIMCORE* will issue an error if rescheduling is attempted within a nested invocation of *gen_int_handler*( ), as this act makes little sense: processes scheduled in this way will be immediately rescheduled again, when control returns to the earlier invocations.

The modules for the special-purpose handlers are *IOSVC*, for I/O monitor calls; *DEVINT*, for device interrupts; *PAGEINT*, for page faults; *PROCSVC*, for process control monitor calls; and *TIMEINT*, for timer interrupts. They are described in the following subsections.

The central *OSP* data structure underlying general interrupt handling is *Int_Vector* (p. 5). The *OSP* data structures that the general interrupt handler will need to "pass along" for special-purpose handling are *IORB* (p. 34), for I/O monitor calls; *DEV_ENTRY* (p. 34), for device interrupts; *PTBR* (p. 6) and *PAGE_TBL* (p. 24), for page faults; and *PCB* (p. 18) and *EVENT* (p. 18), for process control monitor calls.

The interface to module *INTER* is given by the following tables.

Internal Routine	Called By
gen_int_handler ( ); Normally called by *SIMCORE*; may also be called by *MEMORY* in case of a page fault, by *RESOURCES* to signal the release of a resource, by *FILES* to request I/O, by *DEVINT* to signal completion of an I/O, or by *PROTOCOLS* to enforce flow control. This routine determines the cause of the interrupt and calls appropriate interrupt handler.	*SIMCORE*, *MEMORY*, *FILES*, *DEVINT*, *RESOURCES*, *PROTOCOLS*

External Routine	Host Module
extern int get_clock ( ); Used to calculate cpu burst and accumulated cpu time.	*SIMCORE*
extern iosvc_handler (/* iorb */); `/* IORB *iorb;                */` Handles read/write monitor calls.	*IOSVC*
extern devint_handler (/* dev_entry */); `/* DEV_ENTRY *dev_entry;  */` Handles device interrupts: de-queues iorb, unlocks memory page involved in the completed I/O operation, signals event associated with the iorb.	*DEVINT*

extern pagefault_handler(/*pcb,page_id*/);
`/* PCB *pcb;`
`      int page_id;            */`
Handles page faults.
	PAGEINT

extern start_handler (/* pcb */); **extern kill_handler (/* pcb */);** **extern term_handler (/* pcb */);** `/* PCB *pcb;                  */` Called to handle *startsvc/killsvc/termsvc* interrupts, respectively.	*PROCSVC* *PROCSVC* *PROCSVC*

External Routine (continued)	**Host Module**
extern wait_handler `( /* event */ );` `/* EVENT *event; */` Called in response to a *waitsvc* interrupt; suspends the current process.	*PROCSVC*
extern signal_handler `( /* event */ );` `/* EVENT *event; */` Called in case of *sigsvc* interrupts.	*PROCSVC*
extern timeint_handler `( );` Handles timer interrupts; calls *set_timer*( ).	*TIMEINT*
extern dispatch `( );` Gives control of the cpu to one of the processes in the ready queue.	*CPU*

1.5.1 Timer Interrupt Handling – Module *TIMEINT*

The architecture of the simulated machine underlying *OSP* contains an interval timer that is used for process scheduling. Module *SIMCORE* simulates the timer by decrementing its value as simulated time moves forward. When the value of the timer reaches zero, *SIMCORE* initiates a timer interrupt.[1] On exiting the general interrupt handler, a new process is scheduled. The job of *TIMEINT* is to simply reset the timer to the specified value.

Internal Routine	**Called By**
timeint_handler `( );` Handles timer interrupts; calls *set_timer*( ).	*INTER*

External Routine	**Host Module**
extern set_timer `( /* time_quantum */ );` `/* int time_quantum; */` Called by *timeint_handler*( ) to reset the simulated interval timer.	*SIMCORE*

[1] This interrupt may be delayed by 2—3 time units because *SIMCORE* may turn interrupts off while performing other services.

1.5.2 Process Management Monitor Calls – Module *PROCSVC*

Process control interrupts *sigsvc*, *waitsvc*, *killsvc*, *termsvc*, and *startsvc* are handled by *PROCSVC*. The *startsvc* interrupt is generated by the simulator when a new process arrives in the system. The *termsvc* and *killsvc* interrupts are generated when a process terminates normally or abnormally (is killed). Both interrupts are usually due to *SIMCORE*, but *killsvc* may also be initiated by *RESOURCES* to delete deadlocked processes. The kill and terminate handlers must purge all pending, but not active, iorb's associated with the terminated process (*purge_iorbs*( )), release its resources (*giveup_rsrcs*( )), purge its opened sockets (*purge_sockets*( )), and deallocate its memory (*deallocate*( )).

Monitor calls *sigsvc* and *waitsvc* provide an *event-based* facility for synchronizing processes. Any number of processes can wait on a single event E, and signaling that event has the effect of awakening all processes waiting on E. Signaling an event E is done by setting the *event* field of *Int_Vector* to point to E, the *cause* field of *Int_Vector* to *sigsvc*, and calling *gen_int_handler*( ). The general interrupt handler will in turn call *signal_handler*( ), which sets the *happened* flag of the event to *true*, indicating that the event has occurred. The signal handler inserts all processes waiting on E back into the ready queue, using the routine *insert_ready*( ). The *status* field of each such process must then be set to *ready*, and the *pcb→event* pointer to NULL.

Suspending the currently running process, say P, on an event E is done by setting the *event* field of *Int_Vector* to point to E, the *pcb* field of *Int_Vector* to point to P's pcb, and then generating a *waitsvc* interrupt. This invokes *wait_handler*( ), via *gen_int_handler*( ), which checks if the event passed to it as a parameter has already occurred. If so, then it simply returns P to the ready queue. Otherwise, it suspends P by setting the *status* flag of P's pcb to *waiting*, and placing this pcb into the queue associated with the event E. The *pcb→event* pointer is also set to point to E.

Some interrupt handlers set the *status* field of *PCB* to change the status of a process. Namely, *kill_handler*( ) and *term_handler*( ) set the process status to *done*, while *wait_handler*( ) sets it to *waiting*. On the other hand, processes are marked as *ready* or *running* by *insert_ready*( ) and *dispatch*( ) of module *CPU*.

Signal_handler( ) and *start_handler*( ) call *insert_ready*( ) to insert a process into the ready queue—when a process is awakened by the signaling of an event, in the case of *signal_handler*( ); and when a process is newly created, in the case of *start_handler*( ).

Processes and events in *OSP* are represented by the predefined data types *PCB* and *EVENT*:

```
typedef struct event_node EVENT;
struct event_node    {
    int event_id;          /* used by trace facility;     */
                           /* set by simulator            */
    BOOL happened;         /* true, if event has occurred */
    PCB *waiting_q;        /* queue of pcb's suspended    */
                           /* on this event               */
    int *hook;
};

typedef enum { running, ready, waiting, done } STATUS;

typedef struct pcb_node PCB;
struct pcb_node {
    int pcb_id;            /* set by the simulator        */
    int size;              /* process size in bytes;      */
                           /* set by the simulator        */
    int creation_time;     /* set by the simulator        */
    int last_dispatch;     /* last pcb dispatch time      */
    int last_cpuburst;     /* length of prev cpu burst    */
    int accumulated_cpu;   /* accumulated cpu time        */
    PAGE_TBL *page_tbl;    /* ptr to process page table   */
    STATUS status;         /* process status              */
    EVENT *event;          /* event used to suspend pcb   */
    int priority;          /* may be used by scheduler;   */
                           /* user-defined                */
    PCB *next;             /* optional next pcb pointer   */
    PCB *prev;             /* optional prev pcb pointer   */
    int *hook;
};
```

The interface tables for *PROCSVC* now follow:

Internal Routine	Called By
start_handler (pcb); **kill_handler (pcb);** **term_handler (pcb);** `PCB *pcb;` These are used to handle *startsvc/killsvc/termsvc* interrupts; kill and terminate handlers also call *purge_iorbs*( ) of *DEVICES* to remove the pending (but not active) I/O requests of the process in question, *purge_sockets*( ) of *SOCKETS* to remove its opened sockets, *giveup_rsrcs*( ) of *RESOURCES* to release the resources held by the process, and *deallocate*( ) to deallocate its memory; *start_handler*( ) also calls *insert_ready*( ).	*INTER* *INTER* *INTER*
signal_handler (event); `EVENT *event;` Called in case of a *sigsvc* interrupt; wakes processes up by inserting them into the ready queue via calls to *insert_ready*( ).	*INTER*
wait_handler (event); `EVENT *event;` Called in response to a *waitsvc* interrupt; suspends the current process.	*INTER*

External Routine	Host Module
extern deallocate (/* pcb */); `/* PCB *pcb; */` Called by *kill_handler*( ) and *term_handler*( ) to deallocate memory of a terminated process.	*MEMORY*
extern purge_iorbs (/* pcb */); `/* PCB *pcb; */` Called by *kill_handler*( ) and *term_handler*( ) to purge all pending (but not active) iorb's of the terminated process.	*DEVICES*

External Routine (continued)	**Host Module**
extern purge_sockets `( /* pcb */ );` `/* PCB *pcb; */` Called by *kill_handler*( ) and *term_handler*( ) to purge all sockets associated with the terminated process.	*SOCKETS*
extern giveup_rsrcs `( /* pcb */ );` `/* PCB *pcb; */` Called by *kill_handler*( ) and *term_handler*( ) to release all resources held by the terminated process.	*RESOURCES*
extern insert_ready `( /* pcb */ );` `/* PCB *pcb; */` Called by *start_handler*( ) and *signal_handler*( ) to insert processes into the ready queue.	*CPU*

1.5.3 Page Fault Handling – Module *PAGEINT*

Page faults are generated within module *MEMORY* when a reference is made to a virtual page that is not resident in main memory. A page fault may not necessarily be caused by the currently running process; it may also occur due to a device that needs to lock a page that is not in main memory at the time. Therefore, for *pagefault* interrupts, the pcb of the process associated with the interrupt is the one that is explicitly stored in *Int_Vector.pcb* rather than the one found in *PTBR→pcb*. Routine *pagefault_handler*( ) calls *get_page*( ) of *MEMORY* to retrieve the missing page from the drum and to find a suitable frame in main memory in which to insert the page. Page fault handling is described in detail in Section 1.6.

Internal Routine	**Called By**

pagefault_handler `( pcb, page_id );`
`PCB *pcb;`
`int page_id;`
Called in case of a page fault; calls *get_page*( ) to bring the desired page of the current process into the memory.
	INTER

External Routine	Host Module

extern get_page (/* pcb, page_id */);
`/* PCB *pcb;`
`int page_id; */`
Called to bring the desired page in; *get_page*( ) implements the virtual memory management policy by deciding which frames to replace; also saves dirty pages on the drum.
	MEMORY

1.5.4 Device Interrupt Handling – Module *DEVINT*

A device interrupt is generated by *SIMCORE* to signify the completion of an I/O operation on a disk device. In response to such an interrupt, module *DEVINT* will first issue a *sigsvc* interrupt to inform the process that had requested this I/O that the request has now been serviced. *DEVINT* then removes the serviced iorb from the device queue by calling *deq_io*( ) of module *DEVICES*. The routine *deq_io*( ) finds the iorb associated with the interrupting device in the device table (p. 34). The signaling of user processes by *DEVINT* upon interrupts is what realizes asynchronous user I/O in *OSP*. User I/O and device interrupt handling is discussed fully in Section 1.8.

Internal Routine	Called By
devint_handler (dev_entry); `DEV_ENTRY *dev_entry;` De-queues the iorb, unlocks memory pages involved in this I/O operation, and signals the process whose iorb has just been serviced.	*INTER*

External Routine	Host Module
extern deq_io (/* iorb */); `/* IORB *iorb; */` Removes the I/O request from the device queue; submits the next iorb for execution according to the chosen disk scheduling strategy; the device is found in *iorb→dev_id*.	*DEVICES*

External Routine (continued)	**Host Module**
extern gen_int_handler ( ); Called to signal the event of I/O completion and to unblock the process waiting on the event specified in *iorb→event*.	*INTER*

1.5.5 I/O Monitor Calls – Module *IOSVC*

IOSVC handles requests for user I/O. Such request are made by module *FILES* in response to read/write calls to the physical file system. *IOSVC*'s basic task then is to enqueue iorb's to the appropriate device queues. Procedure *enq_io*( ) of module *DEVICES*, which does the actual device scheduling, is called for this purpose. More details on I/O requests can be found in Sections 1.8 and 1.9.

Internal Routine	**Called By**
iosvc_handler `( iorb );` `IORB *iorb;` Handles *read/write* monitor calls; enqueues iorb's.	*INTER*

External Routine	**Host Module**
extern enq_io `( /* iorb */ );` `/* IORB *iorb;  */` Puts the request on the queue of the appropriate device; the device is found in *iorb → dev_id*.	*DEVICES*

1.6 Memory Management – Module *MEMORY*

Virtual memory is a memory management technique that provides the programmer with the convenient illusion of an address space that may be substantially larger than physical main memory. Implicit in such a scheme is that a program need not reside completely in main memory in order to execute.

Paging is a form of virtual memory where user programs are divided into fixed-size units called *pages*, physical memory is divided into fixed-size units called *page frames*, and the size of a page is the same as the size of a frame. It is common to distinguish between the terms *virtual address space*, the pages of a user program, and *physical address space*, the page frames of physical memory.

To implement virtual memory, a fast disk or drum is needed to store an image of the virtual address space of each user process. Furthermore, when a reference to a virtual address is generated by an executing process, the virtual address must be translated into a physical address. Virtual address translation is complicated by the fact that the pages of a process may be scattered anywhere in memory, and some pages may not reside in physical memory at all.

Assuming the referenced virtual page is memory-resident, address translation works basically as follows: the id number of the virtual page is used to index into the *page table* of the executing process, where the id of the frame containing the page can be found. The page table of the currently executing process is pointed to by a special-purpose register known as the *page table base register*. Techniques to speed up address translation include the use of a fast associative memory, in which a subset of the page table entries are stored.

A reference to a virtual page not in physical memory results in a *page fault*. The desired page must be swapped into physical memory from the storage device, possibly replacing a page if all page frames are occupied at the time. Which page to replace is a function of the "page replacement policy" of the memory manager. The page tables of the processes whose pages were swapped in or out this way must be updated to reflect the new state of physical memory.

OSP is designed to support paging in a number of ways. As described in Section 1.2.3, physical memory is divided into *MAX_FRAME* page frames of size *PAGE_SIZE* bytes each. As such, the conversion of a virtual address into a page table index is achieved via integer division of the virtual address by *PAGE_SIZE*. A simulated drum is provided whose swap area is accessible via calls to the *SIMCORE* routine *siodrum*( ). Furthermore, a page table base register, *PTBR*, is available as a global variable. Page tables are represented by a predefined data type of *OSP*:

```
typedef struct page_entry_node PAGE_ENTRY;
struct page_entry_node   {
    int frame_id;       /* frame that holds this page    */
```

```
                               /* set by simulator               */
    BOOL valid;                /* true, if page in main memory   */
    int *hook;
};

typedef struct page_tbl_node PAGE_TBL;
struct page_tbl_node    {
    PCB *pcb;                  /* pcb that owns this page table */
    PAGE_ENTRY page_entry[MAX_PAGE];
    int *hook;
};

int Prepage_Degree;        /* regulates degree of prepaging */
```

Other relevant data types are: *FRAME* (p. 6), *Frame_Tbl* (p. 6), *PTBR* (p. 6), *PCB* (p. 18), *IORB* (p. 34), and *Int_Vector* (p. 5).

Paging works as follows in *OSP*. The simulator simulates an access to virtual memory on behalf of the currently executing process by calling the routine *refer*( ) of this module. It should be emphasized that *refer*( ) simulates a sequence of operations typically performed in *hardware*. A pointer to the page table of the current process is in *PTBR*. A pointer to the pcb of that process can be found in *PTBR→pcb*, as usual.

As described in detail below, the overhead associated with paging can be reduced by implementing a "dirty bit" scheme. This technique requires *refer*( ) to set the dirty bit of the accessed frame whenever the *action* argument indicates that the memory reference may change the contents of memory (*action* = *store*). *Refer*( ) then proceeds to translate the given virtual address to a physical address.

If the desired virtual page is found to be in physical memory then all is well. Otherwise, *refer*( ) initiates a page fault interrupt described later. Note that the page fault handler may call the cpu scheduler, which may in turn assign the cpu to another process. Therefore, after a page fault, *PTBR→pcb* may point to the pcb of another process. So, if the programmer needs to know the pcb of the process that made the memory access (e.g., in order to set the dirty bit on), then *PTBR→pcb* should be saved *before* initiating the page fault interrupt.

If at any time a page becomes involved in an I/O operation, then the *DEVICES* module will lock that page to protect it from being swapped out. *DEVICES* does this by calling *lock_page*( ), which increments the *lock_count* field of the frame holding the page in question. Note that a "count" rather than a "flag" is used because, in principle, a frame may be involved in more than one ongoing I/O operation, if multiple devices start data transfer into or from the frame at about the same time. When the I/O is done, the *DEVICES* module will decrement *lock_count* by calling the *unlock_page*( ) routine. If unlocking is not performed at this point, the simulator will issue a warning. Notice that since the page to be locked must be in main memory, *lock_page*( ) may have to bring the page into memory. As in *refer*( ), this is done by causing a page fault interrupt.

A page fault interrupt can be initiated by setting *Int_Vector.cause* to *pagefault*, *Int_Vector.page_id* to the id of the page that caused the interrupt, *Int_Vector.pcb* to point to the pcb of the process that owns the page, and calling the general interrupt handler.

A call to *gen_int_handler*( ) results in the suspension of the current process and transfer of control to the *PAGEINT* module (the page-fault interrupt handler). *PAGEINT* is passed a pcb and a fault-producing virtual page id and must now come up with a free frame for the referenced virtual page. This is done by calling *get_page*( ), where the page allocation and replacement policies are actually implemented. If a free frame is available, *get_page*( ) copies the desired virtual page from the drum into this frame. Otherwise, *get_page*( ) must select a suitable page to replace and then bring in the desired page. The page to be replaced must reside in a frame with a *lock_count* of 0. The *dirty* flag of the frame should also be checked by *get_page*( ) to see if contents of the frame need to be copied to the drum. The actual page transfer is performed by calling *siodrum*( ) of *SIMCORE* (start I/O on drum).

When a page is sought for replacement, it should be kept in mind that a locked frame cannot be allocated to a new process, even if this frame is marked as free. A free yet locked frame may arise when a process is killed or terminated in the midst of an ongoing I/O operation associated with this process. The consequences of allocating such a frame to another process are highly undesirable, resulting in the phenomenon known as I/O interlock.

Observe that the number of locked frames can never exceed the number of devices. Since the number of devices is much smaller than the number of frames, *SIMCORE* assumes that there always exist unlocked frames that can be used to satisfy the *get_page*( ) request.

Page transfers are not treated in the same way as normal user I/O, as such transfers appear to happen instantaneously.[2] The simulator keeps track of page swaps that occur as a result of calls to *siodrum*( ). It charges the module a certain number of time units for each swap, and produces a report on how much page traffic the virtual memory management scheme is generating.

Dirty bit optimization can be incorporated through the *dirty* flag of the *FRAME* data type. A frame's *dirty* flag should be set to *false* when a page is swapped into it from the drum. It should be set to *true* whenever the page resident in the frame is referenced by *refer*( ) with the *action* argument indicating *store* (from a register into main memory), or by *lock_page*( ), when the *iorb.action* argument indicates *read* (from disk into main memory). The simulator keeps track of the dirty pages to prohibit their overwriting without proper updating of the process image in the swap area. If such overwriting occurs, the simulator generates an error message, and terminates. Even though implementing the "dirty bit" strategy is not mandatory, the simulator issues a warning each time a "clean" page is swapped out, for it considers such a swap redundant.

What we have so far described is demand-paging memory management. The student is also free to implement *prepaging* by trying to anticipate the pages that a process is likely to access when it is dispatched. The standard *OSP* process dispatcher first calls the routine *prepage*( ) of *MEMORY*. If prepaging is not being implemented, then the body of this routine can be left empty, in which case pure demand paging will result.

Exactly how much of a process is to be prepaged may affect the efficiency of the whole system, and is left for the user to decide. For instance, the user may choose to swap in only the "working set" of pages for each process, as in the standard implementation of the *MEMORY* module supplied with *OSP*. To help implement the working set strategy, the routine *get_clock*( ) of *SIMCORE* and the *size* field in the *PCB* data type can be used. The working set of pages can be kept in an array associated with the page table of each process. Do not forget to free the memory occupied by the working set data structure when the process terminates; see *deallocate*( ) below.

A global variable *Prepage_Degree* (ranging from 0 to 10) can be used to regulate the amount of prepaging. This variable is one of the

[2] The illusion of instantaneous page transfer is a simplifying assumption in *OSP*.

simulation parameters; it is set at the beginning of simulation, but can be changed at snapshot breaks. The simulator insists however, that this variable will not be changed under any other circumstances.

Module *MEMORY* also supplies a cost-function associated with prepaging, *start_cost(pcb)*. It returns the cost of executing *prepage(pcb)*, i.e., *COST_OF_PAGE_TRANSFER* times the number of pages that need to be swapped in or out in order to prepage the process represented by *pcb*. The constant *COST_OF_PAGE_TRANSFER* is declared in the heading of the *MEMORY* module. *Start_cost*( ) can be used by the cpu scheduler to decide the priorities of processes. It may return different cost estimates at different times because, depending on the current state of memory, some of the requested pages may already be in memory and some pages of other processes may have to be swapped out.

Procedure *deallocate(pcb)* returns all frames occupied by the process represented by *pcb* to the pool of free frames. A frame is deallocated by clearing its *free* flag and the *valid* flag of the associated page. *Deallocate*( ) is called when a process terminates or is killed; therefore, there is no need to save the newly freed pages on the drum. *Deallocate*( ) does not need to check whether a frame is unlocked since, as explained above, free frames that are locked by ongoing I/O cannot be allocated to other processes anyway. If a student's memory management module maintains dynamic data structures for processes (such as "working sets" of pages), *deallocate*( ) is an ideal place to free the memory allocated to such structures when the associated process terminates.

Internal Routine	Called By
memory_init ( ); Called once to allow for the initialization of internal data structures; the body of this routine can be left empty, if no initialization is needed.	*SIMCORE*
prepage (pcb); `PCB *pcb;` Prepages the process specified in the argument.	*CPU*
int start_cost (pcb); `PCB *pcb;` Calculates the cost of prepaging in terms of the number of pages to be swapped in or out, times the cost of page transfer.	*CPU*

Internal Routine (continued);	**Called By**
deallocate `( pcb );` `PCB *pcb;` Called by the terminate and kill handlers to deallocate pages occupied by the terminated process represented by *pcb*.	*PROCSVC*

get_page `( pcb, page_id );`
`PCB *pcb;`
`int page_id;`
Implements page allocation and replacement; if replacement, decides which frame to replace; brings the desired page into main memory and saves the old frame contents on the drum, if needed; calls *siodrum*( ) of *SIMCORE* to do the actual page transfer; sets valid/invalid and other flags.
	PAGEINT

lock_page `( iorb );` **unlock_page** `( iorb );` `IORB *iorb;` Called to lock/unlock the specified page; memory locking is used to protect pages involved in active I/O operations from being swapped out; locking/unlocking is done by incrementing/decrementing the *lock_count* field of the corresponding frames.	*DEVICES*

refer `( logic_addr, action );`
`int logic_addr;`
`REFER_ACTION action;`
Called by *SIMCORE* to simulate memory access by cpu; *logic_addr* is a logical address within the virtual memory of the current process; it is converted to a physical address using the page table pointed to by *PTBR*; the *action* parameter indicates whether this is a *store* operation, which changes the memory contents, or a *load* operation, which does not; this information is needed for "dirty bit" optimization.
	SIMCORE

External Routine	Host Module

extern siodrum `( /* action, pcb, page_id, frame_id */ );`
`/* IO_ACTION action;`
`PCB *pcb;`
`int page_id, frame_id; */`
Transfers page between main memory and the drum; *action* is either *read* or *write*; with *read*, the page *page_id* is brought from the drum into the frame *frame_id*; with *write* the contents of the frame *frame_id* is saved in the swap area of the process represented by *pcb*, in the block designated for the page *page_id*.
	SIMCORE

extern int get_clock `( );` Returns the current value of the *OSP* clock; can be used to implement the working set page-replacement policies.	*SIMCORE*
extern gen_int_handler `( );` Is called to simulate page faults.	*INTER*

1.7 CPU Scheduling – Module *CPU*

Given a set of processes ready and waiting to execute, cpu scheduling is essentially the task of deciding which of these processes should be allocated the cpu next. The goal of cpu scheduling is to improve cpu utilization, system throughput, response time, and other performance characteristics. Typically, scheduling decisions are made when the cpu is interrupted by an I/O device, a monitor call, or the interval timer. The cpu scheduler decides on the relative priority of processes by looking at characteristics such as age, expected memory and cpu requirements, time of last dispatch, etc.

In *OSP*, cpu scheduling is the function of *CPU*. This module exports the procedures *insert_ready*( ) and *dispatch*( ). Procedure *insert_ready*(*pcb*) inserts *pcb* into the queue of ready processes based on the cpu scheduling algorithm of the *OSP* programmer's choice. It also changes the *status* field of the process to *ready*. Calls to *insert_ready*( ) occur in module *PROCSVC*, when a process is newly created or awakened by a signal.

In *insert_ready*( ), it is advised to verify that the pcb being inserted into the ready queue is not already present in the queue. Depending on the actual implementation of the ready queue, inserting a process twice may disconnect the queue, unintentionally making some ready processes inaccessible. Since these stranded processes can never be rescheduled, statistics such as turnaround time will be adversely impacted.

Procedure *dispatch*( ) is called just before exiting the general interrupt handler. The first thing to do when dispatching a process is to check if another process was running before *dispatch*( ) was called (i.e., *PTBR* $\neq$ NULL and *PTBR*→*pcb*→*status* = *running*). If so, insert this process into the ready queue, otherwise it may never enter the ready queue again, which eventually will lead to a warning or even an error issued by *SIMCORE*.

Procedure *dispatch*( ) must next choose a process in the ready queue, typically the one at the head, to be allocated the cpu. This is effected by updating the global variable *PTBR* to point to the page table of this newly scheduled process (*PTBR* = *current_pcb*→*page_tbl*), and by setting the *status* field of this process's pcb to *running*. If no process is to be run, *PTBR* is set to NULL. It is important to keep *PTBR* up-to-date, since the simulator monitors the contents of this register and will issue a fatal error if it discovers that *PTBR* was not updated appropriately (e.g., if it points to the page table of a waiting process). Just before exiting, the dispatcher sets the pcb field *last_dispatch* of the process to be run next to the value of the current clock, obtained from *get_clock*( ) of *SIMCORE*.

The process that is dispatched can be either *prepaged* into main memory prior to obtaining control of the cpu (by calling *prepage*( ) of *MEMORY*), or pure *demand paging* can be used. In the former case, the cost of the prepaging operation, dependent on how many pages need to be swapped in at the given time, can be determined by calling *start_cost*( ), also of module *MEMORY*. This cost can be used to decide where in the ready queue to insert a process. That is, it may affect the priority of the process.

It should be noted that *SIMCORE* makes no assumptions about the structure of the ready queue, nor about the division of responsibilities between *insert_ready*( ) and *dispatch*( ). The only rule to observe here is that the former must actually insert its argument pcb into the ready queue, while the latter must dispatch some ready process. As a result, a wide variety of scheduling strategies can be implemented within the framework of *OSP*.

The *get_clock*( ) routine of *SIMCORE* and the *creation_time* field of the *PCB* data type can be used to implement "aging"; i.e., the policy of gradually increasing the priority of jobs that have been waiting in the system for long periods of time. The pcb fields *last_dispatch*, *last_cpuburst*, and *accumulated_cpu* can also be used to make priority-based scheduling decisions. When a process is first created, *SIMCORE* initializes *last_dispatch* to a negative number, *last_cpuburst* and *accumulated_cpu* to 0, and *creation_time* to the current value of the simulator clock. The general interrupt handler is responsible for keeping *last_cpuburst* and *accumulated_cpu* up to date (see Section 1.5), while *last_dispatch* is updated by *dispatch*( ). Note that prepaging a process takes time and *SIMCORE* may advance the clock after each *prepage*( ) call. Therefore, the field *last_dispatch* must be set only *after* the process is prepaged; otherwise, the simulator may issue an error if it finds a discrepancy between its own last dispatch time and the student's.

The interval timer of *OSP* allows round-robin-based cpu scheduling algorithms to be implemented. The timer is set using the routine *set_timer*( ) of *SIMCORE*. The simulated hardware decrements the value of the timer with each simulated cpu cycle and, when this value becomes zero, *SIMCORE* generates a timer interrupt.

The global variable *Quantum*, declared below, is an *OSP* simulation parameter that provides a convenient way of adjusting the time quantum used in round robin scheduling. An initial value, specified by the user, is given to *Quantum* by *SIMCORE* at the beginning of simulation. Thereafter, it may be changed at snapshot breaks.[3] Note that, by itself, *Quantum* has no effect on timer interrupts unless it is passed to *set_timer*( ) as a parameter.

```
int Quantum;              /* time quantum for round robin */
```

Other data types relevant to cpu scheduling are: *PCB* (p. 18) and *PTBR* (p. 6).

[3] Actually, *SIMCORE* insists that *Quantum* be changed *only* at snapshot breaks.

Internal Routine	Called By
cpu_init ( ); Called once to allow for the initialization of data structures internal to *CPU*; the body of *cpu_init*( ) can be left empty, if no initialization is needed.	*SIMCORE*
insert_ready (pcb); `PCB *pcb;` Inserts a process into the queue of ready processes according to some scheduling policy.	*PROCSVC*
dispatch ( ); Designates a process to run.	*INTER*

External Routine	Host Module
extern prepage (/* pcb */); **extern int start_cost (/* pcb */);** `/* PCB *pcb; */` *Prepage*( ) prepages the process represented by *pcb*; *start_cost*( ) calculates the cost of prepaging, but does no actual page transfer.	*MEMORY*
extern set_timer (/* time_quantum */); `/* int time_quantum; */` Resets the simulated interval timer; permits round-robin-based scheduling.	*SIMCORE*
extern int get_clock ( ); returns the current simulator clock; can be used to implement "aging" policies.	*SIMCORE*

1.8 Device Management – Module *DEVICES*

The purpose of module *DEVICES* is to manage efficiently the secondary storage devices—disks, in the case of *OSP*. This is accomplished via the judicious scheduling of I/O requests made by processes as they execute in a multi-programmed environment. Since *OSP* is a simulated system, I/O requests are generated "at random" by module *SIMCORE* in the form of read/write commands to the file system module *FILES* (Section 1.9). That is, a user request to read or write a file at a specified position within the file is translated into a request to read or write a block of data at a corresponding disk address. This translation of file positions to disk addresses is performed by the routines *readf*( ) and *writef*( ) of *FILES*.

Disk devices in *OSP* are quite simple: there is only one surface per device, which is divided into a fixed number, *MAX_TRACK*, of concentric tracks. Each track contains the same number of blocks, and a block holds *PAGE_SIZE* bytes. Therefore, in *OSP* the unit of I/O data transfer, the disk block, is the same as the unit of main memory, the page frame. Each track contains a total of *TRACK_SIZE* bytes. *MAX_BLOCK*, the maximum number of blocks on a device, is related to the other constants as follows: $MAX\_BLOCK = MAX\_TRACK \times TRACK\_SIZE/PAGE\_SIZE$. Note that all *OSP* disk devices have the same number of tracks and blocks. In a real system these parameters might vary from device to device, and would thus appear in the entries of the device table. However, *OSP* does not sacrifice much by making this assumption.

A number of algorithms have been proposed for disk scheduling. Their objective is, given a set of outstanding I/O requests, to minimize the total number of tracks traversed by the read/write head of the disk in servicing the requests. The simplest of these algorithms is first-come-first-serve (FCFS). More elaborate approaches include shortest-seek-time-first (SSTF), in which the request closest to the current head position is serviced next; SCAN, where the disk head sweeps from one end of the disk to the other, servicing requests as it goes; and C-SCAN, a variant of SCAN that upon reaching the outer end of the disk immediately returns to the beginning of the disk, without servicing any requests on the return trip. LOOK and C-LOOK are versions of SCAN and C-SCAN, respectively, that move the head only as far as the last request (as opposed to the last track) in each direction.

The main data structure of module *DEVICES* is the *device table*, which contains an entry for each disk device in the system. An important component of a device table entry is the queue of *I/O request blocks* (abbr., *iorb's*), representing the outstanding I/O requests for the device. An iorb is assembled by module *FILES* and added to the iorb queue for the device in question using procedure *enq_io*( ) of this module. Exactly where in the device queue the iorb is inserted depends on the disk scheduling strategy being implemented. Queues of iorb's do not have to be simple linked lists. Efficient implementation of some strategies (e.g., SSTF and LOOK) may require more elaborate indexed structures.

When a device is not in use, the *DEVICES* module can initiate a pending I/O request by calling *siodev*( ) (start I/O device) of *SIMCORE*. The simulator first simulates the I/O and, at some time later, a device interrupt. *SIMCORE* produces the interrupt by first setting the appropriate fields in the interrupt vector data structure and then calling the general interrupt handler, which in turn transfers control to the device interrupt handler (see modules *INTER* and *DEVINT*). The device interrupt handler calls *deq_io*( ) of the *DEVICES* module in order to delete the iorb of the completed I/O operation and to initiate another I/O operation, if at least one request is still pending. *Deq_io*( ) also notifies the file organization module, *FILES*, about completion of I/O by calling *notify_files*( ).

To simplify things slightly, all I/O requests are assumed to involve a single disk block, and thus, since the block size equals the page size, one page of main memory. Naturally, the block id and page id of an I/O request are stored in the request's iorb, along with other pertinent information. Data types for device scheduling are given next.

```
typedef struct dev_entry_node DEV_ENTRY;
struct dev_entry_node   {
    int dev_id;         /* device id - index into Dev_Tbl; */
                        /* set by simulator               */
    BOOL busy;          /* the busy flag; true, if busy   */
    BOOL free_blocks[MAX_BLOCK];
                        /* block i is free if and only if */
                        /* free_blocks[i] = true          */
    IORB *iorb;         /* iorb serviced by this device   */
    int *dev_queue;     /* optional ptr to device queue   */
    int *hook;
};

DEV_ENTRY Dev_Tbl[MAX_DEV];

typedef struct iorb_node IORB;
struct iorb_node   {
    int iorb_id;        /* used by the trace facility;    */
```

```
                       /* set by simulator                  */
    int dev_id;        /* assoc'd dev; index into Dev_Tbl  */
    IO_ACTION action;  /* read or write                     */
    int block_id;      /* block involved in the I/O         */
    int page_id;       /* buffer page in main memory        */
    PCB *pcb;          /* pcb that issued the request       */
    EVENT *event;      /* event to be used to synch I/O     */
    OFILE *file;       /* assoc'd entry in open file tbl    */
    IORB *next;        /* optional next iorb in dev queue   */
    IORB *prev;        /* optional prev iorb in dev queue   */
    int *hook;
};
```

Other relevant data types are: *EVENT* (p. 18), *PCB* (p. 18), and *OFILE* (p. 39).

The fields in the above data types are mostly self-explanatory, but a few comments are in order. Track numbers on a device range from 0 to $MAX\_TRACK - 1$. A device number *dev_id* is an index into the device table, *Dev_Tbl*, and ranges from 0 to $MAX\_DEV - 1$. The field *free_blocks* in *DEV_ENTRY* is a bit-vector of free space on the device. It indicates which blocks of the device are free (*free_blocks*[i] = *true*) and which are not (= *false*). More details on disk storage allocation can be found in the section on file organization, Section 1.9.

Observe that the *IORB* data type refers to the disk block involved in an I/O operation rather than the track. Therefore, when implementing policies such as LOOK or SSTF, the user has to convert block numbers into track numbers using the aforesaid constants *TRACK_SIZE* and *PAGE_SIZE*. It should be noted that *SIMCORE* is unable to differentiate between LOOK and SCAN, and C-LOOK and C-SCAN; although each of these strategies is acceptable, the statistics generated by *SIMCORE* will be those for LOOK and C-LOOK, respectively. Furthermore, *SIMCORE* assumes that at the very beginning each device's disk head is positioned at track 0.

To guard against the problem of I/O interlock, where a page frame involved in an ongoing I/O operation is accessed unwittingly by another process, any page frame that is the target of an active I/O operation must be locked. This is accomplished by calling the *lock_page*( ) procedure of *MEMORY* just prior to starting the actual data transfer, i.e., before the call to *siodev*( ). Procedure *unlock_page*( ) has the opposite effect on memory; it is called by *deq_io*( ) when an I/O operation has completed.

Note that an iorb contains the *virtual* address of the buffer in main memory from which the data is to be read or written. This corresponds to the Direct Virtual Memory Access (DVMA) I/O architecture used in some advanced computer systems such as the SUN-3 workstation. Older architectures, such as the IBM 370, use Direct Memory Access (DMA) I/O, which requires *physical* main memory addresses in iorb's. Using DVMA in *OSP*, as well as in the SUN-3 architecture, leads to simpler and cleaner I/O software.

User I/O in *OSP* is asynchronous: the execution of a user program may continue asynchronously after a read/write command has been issued. This is made possible by the fact that each I/O operation is associated with an event (see the read/write commands of *FILES*) on which the user process can synchronize in order to test the completion of the specified I/O operation. Events are discussed more fully in Section 1.5.2. As a result, a device queue may contain more than one iorb from the same process.

The routine *purge_iorbs*( ) is called from module *PROCSVC* when a process terminates or is killed. This routine removes all pending iorb's associated with the process. However, it should not remove iorb's associated with ongoing I/O operations, as these operations cannot be interrupted. Note that for the iorb's that are removed, the associated I/O operations are never initiated; therefore the main memory pages referred to by these iorb's need not be unlocked—they were never locked in the first place. Also, for each iorb purged from a device queue, *purge_iorbs*( ) must make a call to *notify_files*( ) of module *FILES* to let it know that the corresponding I/O request will not be serviced. Since only the process that owns an iorb can wait on the event associated with the iorb, signaling this event is not necessary when the process terminates or is killed.

For each device, the user must keep track of when it is free or busy. It is an error to start a busy device, while leaving a device idle when its queue is non-empty will result in a warning. Initially all devices are assumed idle. Subsequently, a device becomes busy when an *siodev*( ) command is executed on that device. The completion of an I/O operation on a device triggers a *devint* interrupt, which is propagated to module *DEVICES* via a call to *deq_io*( ) by the device interrupt handler.

Internal Routine	Called By
devices_init ( ); Allows for the initialization of data structures internal to *DEVICES*; the body of this routine can be left empty, if no initialization is needed.	*SIMCORE*
enq_io (iorb); IORB *iorb; Enqueues I/O requests to devices.	*IOSVC*
deq_io (iorb); IORB *iorb; Called by the device interrupt handler when the device whose id is found in *iorb→dev_id* is done; it de-queues the iorb and submits the next one for execution; *iorb* is the iorb serviced by the device.	*DEVINT*
purge_iorbs (pcb); PCB *pcb; Called by the kill and terminate handlers to remove all pending (but not active) iorb's when a process is killed or terminates.	*PROCSVC*

External Routine	Host Module
extern siodev (/* iorb */); /* IORB *iorb; */ Starts the I/O specified in the iorb.	*SIMCORE*
extern lock_page (/* iorb */); **extern unlock_page** (/* iorb */); /* IORB *iorb; */ Called by *enq_io*( )/*deq_io*( ) to lock/unlock the page specified in *iorb*.	*MEMORY* *MEMORY*
extern notify_files (/* iorb */); /* IORB *iorb; */ Called by *purge_iorbs*( ) to inform *FILES* that the *iorb* has been purged and will not be serviced; or by *deq_io*( ) to notify *FILES* about completion of the I/O operation associated with the *iorb*.	*FILES*

1.9 File Organization – Module *FILES*

Module *FILES* implements the file system of *OSP*. To keep things simple, a flat directory structure consisting of a single directory is used. This is in contrast to the hierarchical file structures of systems such as UNIX [4] and MS-DOS. Standard file system commands are provided by *FILES*, including *openf*( ), *closef*( ), *readf*( ), and *writef*( ). Besides manipulating the directory structure, these commands maintain a table of open files and manage the storage space for files on the simulated disk devices of *OSP*.

All information needed to access a file is kept in an *i-node* data structure associated with the file. A file's i-node can be found via the directory: given the name (a character string) of a file, the directory should provide fast retrieval of the file's i-node from the disk where the file is stored.

The purpose of the open file table is to provide fast access to an in-memory copy of an opened file's i-node. It also allows a file, say F, to be independently opened by different processes at the same time. Each such opening of F will correspond to an entry in the open file table, and each of these entries will point to the i-node of F. Our usage of i-nodes and the open file table is pretty much in the spirit of UNIX. Unlike UNIX, *OSP* does not maintain permanent files: files are created and deleted anew with each session with the simulator.

As described in Section 1.8, each disk device is represented as an entry in the device table. For file organization, the relevant field within a device table entry is the free-space bit-vector: *free_blocks*[i] is set to *true* if and only if block i of the corresponding disk is free. Keeping this bit-vector current is one of the tasks of the *FILES* module. The *OSP* type definitions for file organization now follow.

```
typedef struct file_dir_entry_node FILE_DIR_ENTRY;
struct file_dir_entry_node   {
    char *filename;
    INODE *inode;
    int *hook;
};
```

[4] UNIX is a registered trademark of AT&T Bell Laboratories.

```
typedef struct inode_node INODE;
struct inode_node    {
    int inode_id;     /* set by programmer (optional)        */
    int dev_id;       /* device id; index into Dev_Tbl       */
    int filesize;
    int count;        /* # open files assoc'd with i-node */
    int allocated_blocks[MAX_BLOCK];
                      /* info on where file is stored        */
    int *hook;
};

typedef struct ofile_node OFILE;
                       /* entry in table of open files       */
struct ofile_node    {
    int ofile_id;      /* used by the trace facility;        */
                       /* set by simulator                   */
    int dev_id;        /* device where the file resides      */
    int iorb_count;    /* # of this file's pending iorb's */
    INODE *inode;      /* pointer to this file's i-node      */
    int *hook;
};
```

Other relevant data types are: *EVENT* (p. 18), *PCB* (p. 18), *IORB* (p. 34), *PTBR* (p. 6), *PAGE_TBL* (p. 24), *Int_Vector* (p. 5), *DEV_ENTRY* (p. 34), and *Dev_Tbl* (p. 34).

Note that although the formats of directory entries, open file table entries, and i-nodes are predefined in *OSP*, the actual structure of the file directory, open file table, and i-node pool are left to the programmer to decide. In the case of the directory, a search tree or hash table should be used to provide efficient access to a file's i-node.

We now describe the routines exported by *FILES*. In *OSP*, the simulator does not explicitly issue requests for the creation or deletion of files. Instead, when a file is opened for the first time, it is created, and when it is closed for the last time, it is deleted. Therefore, routines for file creation and deletion are not part of the module's interface.

Procedure *openf*( ) has two parameters: *filename*, a character string, and *file*, an entry in the open file table. The second parameter, of type *OFILE*, is allocated by the simulator and passed to *openf*( ) in template form. It will be the responsibility of *openf*( ) to fill in the template. *Openf*( ) first searches the file directory for *filename*. If the file is not found it calls a file creation procedure. This procedure is not called by the routines outside of *FILES*, and thus is not part of the interface table; its format is determined by the student or by the instructor. Guidelines for writing a file creation procedure appear below.

After checking the directory for *filename*, and creating an entry for it if not found, *openf*( ) initializes the *OFILE* template. This is done by setting the *inode* field to point to the appropriate i-node, copying the relevant information from that i-node into the template, and setting the field *iorb_count* to 0. The i-node associated with the file is either found in the directory, if the file already exists, or is otherwise a by-product of the file creation procedure. Note that the device id, *dev_id*, must be recorded in the *OFILE* parameter, even though it also appears in *inode*.[5] *Openf*( ) then increments the *count* field of the file's i-node by 1, and exits. *SIMCORE* assumes that file can always be opened, since, as in UNIX, *openf*( ) creates a file if it does not exist.[6]

Procedure *closef*( ) disconnects the *OFILE* entry for the file from the open file table and decrements the *count* of the file's i-node by one. If the resulting value is zero, then *closef*( ) executes a file deletion procedure (which, again, is not part of the interface).

It is possible that the file to be closed still has unserviced iorb's, which should not go unserviced. Therefore, *closef*( ) checks the number of pending iorb's associated with the file. If pending iorb's exist, then the file is not closed and *fail* is returned; otherwise the file is closed and *ok* is returned. The number of unserviced iorb's for a file is a field in the *OFILE* data structure. It is incremented by *readf*( ) and *writef*( ), and decremented by *notify_files*( ). The latter routine is called by *DEVICES* each time an I/O operation is completed or when an iorb is purged from a device queue.

File creation/deletion procedures may vary depending on the specific requirements of the instructor. However, the following guidelines should be followed. To create a new file, it is necessary to create a new *INODE* and a new *FILE_DIR_ENTRY*. The i-node is initialized by choosing a device, and by setting the *filesize* and *count* fields to 0. Choice of device may depend on several different criteria: storage avail-

---

[5] In real systems, fields such as *filesize* and *allocated_blocks* are also likely to be duplicated in OFILE.

[6] In UNIX, the conditions under which a file cannot be opened are rare, and do not arise in *OSP*.

ability, space allocation strategy, and so on. All information relevant to this decision can be found in *Dev_Tbl*. File deletion frees the blocks occupied by the file (found in the i-node of the file), returns its i-node to the pool of i-nodes, and deletes its entry in the directory.

The array *inode→allocated_blocks* stores information about the disk blocks allocated to a file. This information allows one to transform logic addresses within the file into physical addresses on the device.

Procedures *readf*( ) and *writef*( ) first fill in the iorb template passed as an argument by the simulator. The iorb template is uninitialized, except that *iorb→event* points to a valid *EVENT* data structure, which is also a template. The event template must be initialized by setting the *happened* field to *false* and the *waiting_q* field to NULL. The user process that called *readf*( )/*writef*( ) may continue asynchronously, and later suspend itself on the iorb event if it reaches a point where it needs the result of the call. This event will be signaled by $\mathcal{DEVINT}$ upon completion of the associated I/O operation.

To initialize the iorb template, *readf*( )/*writef*( ) must find the pcb of the process that requested the read/write. Since this process must be the current one, its pcb can be accessed via the page table base register (*PTBR→pcb*). The physical address on the disk needed in the iorb is obtained by translating the *position* argument of *readf*( )/*writef*( ) into a block id using the information in *inode→allocated_blocks*. It should be remembered that a track consists of a whole number of blocks (of size PAGE_SIZE bytes), and a block is the unit of data transfer. Thus, each call to *readf*( ) or *writef*( ) affects only one block. Having finished the assembly of the iorb, these routines increment the number of pending iorb's associated with the file. Eventually, they generate an interrupt, in the form of an I/O monitor call, to place the iorb in the device queue. They return *ok* in case of a success, and *fail* if the *position* is out of range (see later) or if the device does not have enough room (in case of *writef*( )). In case of failure, *readf*( )/*writef*( ) do not cause an interrupt, but simply exit, returning control back to the simulator.

The interrupt corresponding to an I/O monitor call is effected by setting *Int_Vector* to point to the appropriate *IORB*, setting the *cause* to *iosvc*, and then calling *gen_int_handler*( ). The general interrupt handler will pass control to module $\mathcal{IOSVC}$, which in turn calls *enq_io*( ) of $\mathcal{DEVICES}$. The student must be aware of the fact that the cpu scheduler may be called as part of interrupt processing. Therefore, the running processes before and after the interrupt may be different. If the program still needs the pcb of the process that was running before the interrupt occurred, this pcb must be saved for later use.

Procedure *readf*( ) always reads the entire block containing within its range the file position indicated by the *position* argument. If the position is out of range, *readf*( ) returns *fail*. For *readf*( ), the position is considered to be within range if $0 \leq position < inode.filesize$. Notice that file positions start from 0 and end at $filesize - 1$.

Procedure *writef*( ) places data in the block containing the file position within its range. If this reference is pointing past the end of file, the file is expanded by the appropriate number of blocks. To explain, let the position argument to *writef*( ) have the value x. This means that the reference is made to block number $b = \lfloor \frac{x}{PAGE\_SIZE} \rfloor$ of the file (block numbers start with 0). The number of the last block in the file is $b\_last = \lfloor \frac{filesize-1}{PAGE\_SIZE} \rfloor$. If $b > b\_last$ then $b - b\_last$ new blocks will have to be allocated to the file to satisfy the request. *Writef*( ) returns *fail* if either the current reference is out of range (which, for *writef*( ), means that $position < 0$) or if there is no room on the disk to expand the file.

Like the creation and deletion routines, storage allocation is a local procedure whose format is not prescribed by *OSP*. In order to find free blocks on a device, it examines the device's *free_blocks* bit-vector in the device table. Having found enough room, it updates the arrays *inode→allocated_blocks* and $Dev\_Tbl[dev\_id].free\_blocks$ to reflect the new blocks assigned to the file. Any correct storage allocation strategy will be tolerated by *SIMCORE*, provided that no file spans more than one device. However, the simulator will issue a warning whenever it believes that the device has enough room, while the storage allocation strategy claims otherwise (i.e., *writef*( ) returns *fail*).

Internal Routine	Called By
files_init ( ); Allows for the initialization of internal data structures; the body of this routine can be left empty, if no initialization is needed.	*SIMCORE*

openf(filename, file);
`char *filename;`
`OFILE *file;`
Opens the file by filling in the *OFILE*-template *file*. Creates the file, if it did not exist before.
	SIMCORE

Internal Routine (continued)	**Called By**
EXIT_CODE closef(file); `OFILE *file;` Returns *fail* if the file is not closed (because of associated pending I/O); otherwise returns *ok*.	*SIMCORE*
EXIT_CODE readf(file, position, page_id, iorb);	*SIMCORE*

EXIT_CODE writef(file, position, page_id, iorb);
`OFILE *file;`
`int position, page_id;`
`IORB *iorb;`
These routines fill in the *iorb* template supplied by the simulator and then cause an I/O interrupt; *fail* is returned if the I/O operation cannot be performed. *Position* is the position within the file for this I/O request; *page_id* is the main memory page address where the data is to be input/output.
	SIMCORE

notify_files (iorb); `IORB *iorb;` Decrements the number of pending iorb's associated with the file; called by *deq_io*( ) or *purge_iorbs*( ).	*DEVICES*

External Routine	**Host Module**
extern gen_int_handler ( ); Called to place an I/O request.	*INTER*

1.10 Resource Management – Module *RESOURCES*

In a multi-programmed system, processes compete for access to the resources of the system, e.g., cpu cycles, memory space, files, I/O devices, etc. This can result in *deadlock*: a circular wait among a set of processes, each waiting for a resource held by another process in the set. Implicit in this definition is that the resources are non-sharable and that no process is willing to relinquish a resource before its request for additional allocation is satisfied.

The purpose of module *RESOURCES* is to manage the allocation of resources to user processes. To effectively deal with the problem of deadlock, either of two methods can be implemented: *deadlock detection*, where from time to time the system state is checked for the existence of a deadlock; and *deadlock avoidance*, where resources are allocated in such a way as to render deadlock impossible. The global variable *Deadlock_Method*, whose declaration appears below, determines which strategy is being used. Its value is entered as one of the simulation parameters, and can be changed during snapshot breaks. The simulator insists, however, that this variable not be changed under any other circumstances.

In the case of deadlock detection, a *deadlock recovery* algorithm should be executed when a deadlock is detected. Recovery techniques include killing one or more processes in order to break the circular wait, or preempting resources from one or more of the deadlocked processes. The former technique is the one of choice for *RESOURCES*.

Within *OSP*, we will not be concerned with the exact nature of resources. Rather, they are abstract entities created by *SIMCORE*. All the information module *RESOURCES* needs to know about a resource can be found in the global data structure *Resource_Tbl*; e.g., the total number of instances of the resource in the system, the number of instances currently available, and a flag indicating whether or not the resource is sharable. A sharable resource cannot lead to a deadlock, while a non-sharable one can. Note that the simulator will issue a warning each time a request for a sharable resource is denied.

To implement a resource management policy, the student must keep track of how many *instances* of each resource are currently allocated to each active process. These numbers must be updated when *acquire*( ) and *release*( ) are called, the primary procedures exported by *RESOURCES*. In constructing a data structure that reflects the current state of resource allocation, it is useful to know that the number of active pcb's in the system cannot exceed the global constant *MAX_PCB*. It should be noted, however, that the ids of these pcb's can be arbitrarily large and so pcb ids cannot be used for indexing into the resource allocation data structure (but they can be used for hashing).

User requests for resources take the form of simulator-generated calls to *acquire*( ). When a request occurs, module *RESOURCES* must determine if the request can be satisfied. This decision depends on the policy being used. For deadlock detection, a request can be satisfied if the number of free resource instances is sufficient. For deadlock avoidance, the decision-making process may be more involved. For example, to guarantee that a deadlock will never occur, the well-known banker's algorithm uses information about the maximum number of instances of each resource type that a process may ever need.

A request is represented as a *resource request block* (rrb). *SIMCORE* supplies an rrb with each call to *acquire*( ). If an *acquire*( ) request can be satisfied, the resource allocation data structure should be updated by decreasing the number of free instances of the resource type allocated. If a request cannot be satisfied, the rrb is appended to a list in the entry for the resource in the resource table. The process that issued the request is suspended by means of a *waitsvc* interrupt on an event contained in the rrb. More precisely, the rrb points to an *EVENT* data structure created by the simulator. Before generating the *waitsvc* interrupt, *acquire*( ) must initialize the event by setting the *happened* flag to *false*. Note that only the process that owns the rrb can be suspended on the rrb's event.

The *waitsvc* interrupt always suspends the currently running process and ignores the field *pcb* in the data structure *Int_Vector*. One must ensure that this is indeed the process that issued the resource request. If another interrupt occurred between entry to *acquire*( ) and the *waitsvc* interrupt, it is possible that a different process has gained control of the cpu. The pcb of the process that called *acquire*( ), pointed to by *PTBR→pcb* at the moment *acquire*( ) was entered, should be saved to guard against the problem of suspending the wrong process. Event-related interrupts are described more fully in Section 1.5.2.

As alluded to above, the resource manager may need to know the maximal needs of a process to implement deadlock avoidance. This information is provided in the rrb as field *max_need*. The first time a process tries to acquire a resource, its maximal needs for all resources can be found in the rrb parameter to *acquire*( ). In subsequent calls to *acquire*( ) by this process, the field *max_need* can be ignored.

Procedure *release*( ), also called by the simulator, should increase the number of free resource instances and examine the list of rrb's attached to the resource. If one can now be satisfied, which again depends on the strategy being implemented, it decreases the number of free resources, and signals the rrb's event via a *sigsvc* interrupt. The predefined data types for resource management are the following.

```
typedef struct rrb_node RRB;
struct rrb_node   {
    int rrb_id;         /* set by simulator                    */
    PCB *pcb;           /* the requesting process              */
    RESOURCE *rsrc;     /* the requested resource              */
    int quantity;       /* requested quantity                  */
    int max_need[MAX_RSRC];
                        /* max need for each resource;         */
                        /* used with deadlock avoidance        */
    EVENT *event;       /* event to signal when                */
                        /* this request is fulfilled           */
    RRB *next;          /* optional next rrb in rsrc queue */
    RRB *prev;          /* optional prev rrb in rsrc queue */
    int *hook;          /* user can hook anything here         */
};

typedef struct resource_node RESOURCE;
struct resource_node   {
    int rsrc_id;        /* set by simulator; used for          */
                        /* indexing into the resource tbl   */
    int total_qty;      /* tot # of this rsrc's instances   */
    int avail_qty;      /* # of available rsrc's instances */
    BOOL sharable;      /* true if sharable; else false        */
    RRB *rrb;           /* queue of rrb's to this resource */
    int *hook;
};

RESOURCE Resource_Tbl[MAX_RSRC];

typedef enum   {
     avoidance, detection
}           DEADLOCK_TYPE;

DEADLOCK_TYPE Deadlock_Method;
                        /* detection or avoidance              */
```

Other relevant data types are: *PCB* (p. 18), *PTBR* (p. 6), *PAGE_TBL* (p. 24), and *EVENT* (p. 18).

To trigger a deadlock detection procedure, a call to *get_clock*( ) of *SIMCORE* can be used. The clock can be checked on each call to *acquire*( ), and if enough time has elapsed since the previous check, deadlock detection can be initiated. In deadlock detection mode, *SIMCORE* prints a message whenever it detects a deadlock. In deadlock avoidance, deadlocks should not occur, and therefore *SIMCORE* will issue an error if it finds a deadlock.

In conjunction with deadlock detection, students need to implement a deadlock recovery algorithm. In *OSP*, deadlocks can be removed by killing one or more of the processes involved in the deadlock. Processes are killed by generating a *killsvc* interrupt.

Finally, the routine *giveup_rsrcs*( ), which takes the single argument *pcb*, releases all resources held by the process represented by *pcb*. This routine is called by the kill and terminate interrupt handlers of *PROCSVC*. After releasing the resources, *giveup_rsrcs*( ) should attempt to satisfy a pending resource request, signaling the appropriate process if successful. Note, however, that the event associated with an rrb owned by the killed or terminated process should not be signaled, as no other process can be awakened by this event.

Internal Routine	Called By
resources_init ( ); Called once by the simulator to allow for the initialization of data structures internal to *RESOURCES*; the body of this routine can be left empty, if no initialization is needed.	*SIMCORE*
EXIT_CODE acquire (rrb); `RRB *rrb;` Returns *ok* if the request is granted.	*SIMCORE*

release (rsrc, qty);
`RESOURCE *rsrc;`
`int qty;`
Releases specified number of resource instances.
	SIMCORE

giveup_rsrcs (pcb); `PCB *pcb;` Called by *kill_handler*( ) and *term_handler*( ) to release all resources held by a process.	*PROCSVC*

External Routine	Host Module
extern gen_int_handler ( ); Called by *acquire*( ) to produce a *waitsvc* interrupt and suspend a process, or to produce a *killsvc* interrupt and kill processes entangled in a deadlock; it is also called by *release*( ) to signal the release of resources.	*INTER*
extern int get_clock ( ); Returns the current time; can be used to trigger deadlock detection.	*SIMCORE*

1.11 Interprocess Communication – Module *SOCKETS*

A *socket* is a bidirectional port that a process creates in order to send and receive messages. A socket normally has a name or an address bound to it. A process can specify that a connection be established between a local socket that it has created (the so-called *host* socket) and a socket belonging to another process (the *peer* socket); it need only know the name of the peer socket. After establishing the connection, the processes are free to exchange messages.

Sockets evolved due to extensive research among the UNIX 4.2BSD design team to address the lack of an adequate interprocess communication facility in earlier versions of UNIX. Prior to sockets, the standard mechanism used was the *pipe*, which requires processes wishing to communicate to have a common parent process; pipes thus support only intramachine communication. Sockets, on the other hand, support communication between any two processes, independent of their location. In fact, in UNIX 4.2BSD, pipes have been implemented through sockets.

The purpose of module *SOCKETS* is to implement a simplified, yet realistic version of UNIX sockets. We begin with a brief overview of UNIX sockets, and then discuss our simplifications. The main reference source for our presentation of sockets, and of protocols given in the next section, is the text *The Design and Implementation of the 4.3BSD*

UNIX Operating System, by Samuel J. Leffler, Marshall K. McKusick, Michael J. Karels and John S. Quarterman, Addison-Wesley, 1989.

Sockets provide a uniform and convenient interface for communicating messages between processes, one that is independent of the underlying hardware; e.g., the physical network. The actual communication is carried out by the *protocols*, the subject of Section 1.12. This separation of concerns is reflected in the layered manner in which sockets are implemented: user requests come into the socket layer but are serviced at the protocol layer. Protocols can be added or deleted without affecting the socket-layer interface to user processes. This layered approach is similar to the one used in the implementation of the file system: read/write commands to the file system are independent of the physical nature of the devices where the files are stored; the actual I/O is the responsibility of the device management module.

It is important to realize that a peer socket may not reside on the same machine as the host socket, and thus cannot be directly manipulated by the host socket's machine. The peer socket's machine may even run a different operating system! One can therefore form the following picture about communication between sockets: A user process asks the socket layer to send a message from a host socket to a peer socket. The socket layer processes the request by updating a data structure associated with the host socket, and then asks the protocol layer to do the dirty work. The protocol layer, being aware of the specifics of the network, selects an appropriate "vehicle" (protocol) to carry out the communication. The message is delivered to the peer socket, provided that the peer socket has enough space in its input buffer to accommodate the message. Otherwise, the message is queued, usually at the sending socket.[7] A schematic view of the relationship between the socket and protocol layers appears in Figure 1.2.

Sockets come in various flavors. Two important ones are *stream* and *datagram* sockets. Stream sockets provide bidirectional, reliable and sequenced communication, without loss of data or duplication. They do not preserve message boundaries. Stream sockets require an explicit connection to be made before sending or receiving data. Datagram sockets do not guarantee reliable communication. Messages may be lost,

[7] In intermachine communication, messages sometimes travel via intermediate sockets, in which case a message may be queued at an intermediate socket, if the destination socket cannot accept the message.

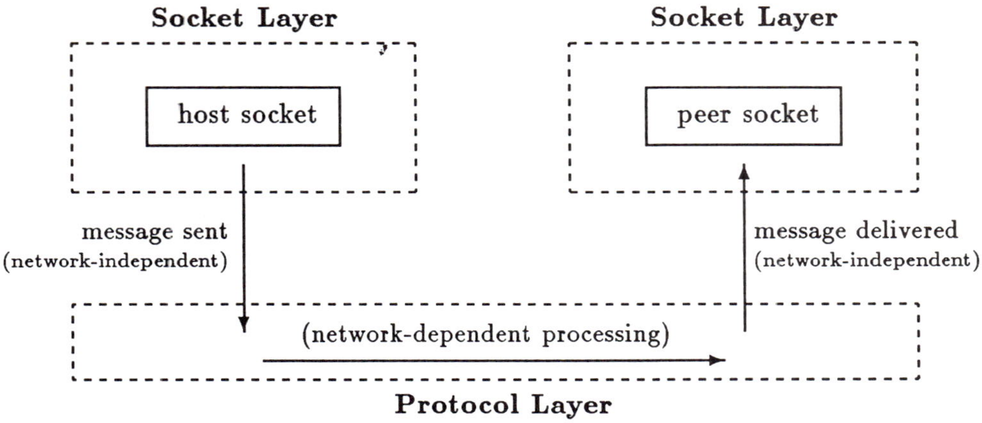

FIGURE 1.2 Communication between Sockets

duplicated, or may arrive out of order. However, message boundaries are preserved—messages are queued at the receiving socket, each message being held in a special datagram message buffer designed specifically to preserve message boundaries. Datagram sockets do not require establishing a connection before sending or receiving data.

Associated with a socket is the *communication domain* in which it lives. A communication domain defines a family of protocols, normally one per socket type, that is suited to a particular communication architecture (communication domains are organization- or vendor-specific). Consequently, communication domains also define the format of socket addresses. The two most well-known domains are the UNIX domain for intramachine communication, and the Internet domain for communication across networks. The name format for the UNIX domain is ordinary file system paths, such as */usr/local/news.cs*. Processes communicating in the Internet domain use Internet addresses (names), which consist of 32-bit host number and a 32-bit port number, and the DARPA Internet protocol family (TCP/IP for stream sockets and UDP for datagram sockets).

Stream sockets are commonly used in a client/server mode of communication. Consider a server process, such as a file server or a yellow-pages server; the latter provides clients with addresses of other servers. The server process first opens a socket, say s, and binds a name to *s*, say *SERVSOC*, such that *SERVSOC* is known globally throughout the network. The server then uses *s* in a *listen* command to receive connection requests from potential client processes. For each incoming connection request, the server may issue an *accept* command, with *s* as a parameter, to create a new socket connected to a socket in the client process. To complete the picture, the server usually forks off a process to manage the just-completed connection to the client.

At the other end, a process in need of *SERVSOC*'s service creates a socket for itself, say *r*, and issues a *connect* command with *r* and *SERVSOC* as parameters. If successful, the client will now be able to communicate with *SERVSOC* using its local socket *r*. The server may reside anywhere in the network and it is a function of the protocol layer to locate it and initiate the connection.

In UNIX, sockets are implemented as part of the file system so that they appear pretty much like files to processes. When a socket is created, a socket descriptor, which resembles a UNIX file descriptor, is returned, and can be used in subsequent socket system calls. A socket descriptor serves as an index into the per-process open file table; a field in the i-node structure identifies the socket as a special file. In this way, applications can use the standard file system calls in conjunction with socket-specific calls.

1.11.1 Representation of Sockets in *OSP*

The socket facility of *OSP* has been designed in the spirit of UNIX, with a number of simplifications. First, the socket interface is separate from that of the file system. Besides being consistent with the modular construction of *OSP*, this separation allows the file system and the socket facility to be assigned as independent projects. Second, since *OSP* simulates only one machine, there is only one communication domain: the *OSP* domain (cf. UNIX domain) for intramachine communication. Within the *OSP* domain, there is exactly one protocol for stream sockets (*PR_STREAM*) and one for datagram sockets (*PR_DGRAM*). The proper protocol is automatically chosen for a given socket type. Finally, there is no *listen* command in *SOCKETS*. A server process explicitly creates a host socket, which it then provides as a parameter to *accept*( ), for each server/client connection.

Since *OSP* currently supports only intramachine communication, one could argue that just one layer, the socket layer, instead of two layers is enough. However, the layered approach discussed above provides a more realistic picture of a modern interprocess communication facility. The enumeration types used by the socket layer follow first.

```
typedef enum  { stream,dgram } SO_TYPE;
typedef enum  { send,recv,accept,recvfrom } SO_ACTION;
```

Other relevant enumeration types used by the socket layer are: *BOOL* (p. 6) and *EXIT_CODE* (p. 6).

Module *SOCKETS* is responsible for handling socket system calls issued by the simulator, namely: *sockets_init*( ), to initialize the protocol switch structures (explained below); *get_so_name*( ), to retrieve the character string representing the name of a socket; *open_sock*( ), to create a socket; *close_sock*( ), to close a socket; *accept_sock*( ), to mark a stream socket as accepting a connection; *connect_sock*( ), to establish a connection between two stream sockets; *send_sock*( ) and *recv_sock*( ), to communicate data between two stream sockets; *sendto_sock*( ) and *recvfrom_sock*( ), to communicate messages between two datagram sockets; and finally *purge_sockets*( ), to remove the open sockets of a terminated process.

A socket is defined by the *SOCKET* data type, which is conceptually similar to a combination of the *INODE* and *OFILE* data types of module *FILES*.

```
typedef struct socket_node SOCKET;
struct socket_node  {
    int so_id;            /* used by trace facility;      */
                          /* set by simulator             */
    SO_TYPE so_type;      /* socket type: stream/dgram    */
    BOOL is_connected;    /* true, if connected           */
    BOOL is_accepting;    /* true, if accepts connections */
    PCB *pcb;             /* pcb that owns this socket    */
    int so_inbuf;         /* buffer for incoming data     */
    int num_msg;          /* only for dgram sockets       */
    DGRAM_BUF *dgram_msg_list;
    PR_SW *pr_sw;         /* protocol switch-struct ptr   */
    PRRB *prrb;           /* protocol request block ptr   */
    BOOL so_error;        /* indicates error, if any;     */
                          /* e.g., when peer terminates   */
    int *hook;            /* user can hook anything here  */
};
```

Many of the fields in *SOCKET* data types are self-explanatory, but several comments are in order. Regarding the field *so_type*, *SIMCORE* will randomly choose a socket type when it calls *open_sock*( ) to create a new socket. The flow of data in *OSP* is simulated only—no data is actually exchanged. As such, the integer *so_inbuf* is used to indicate the amount of data in a socket's input buffer, while the contents of the buffer are left unspecified. This field is updated whenever data is added to or removed from the socket. The size of the buffer is limited to the constant *MAX_DATA*.

The Boolean variables *is_connected* and *is_accepting* are peculiar to stream sockets, which must establish a connection before sending or receiving data. As described above, processes communicate via stream sockets using a client/server model of communication. The server creates a socket for itself and calls *accept_sock*( ) to indicate that it is willing to accept a connection request. The *is_accepting* field will be set to *true* at that time. Later, a client process may issue a connection request, which can be satisfied since *is_accepting* is *true* at the server. Once the two sockets are connected, *is_connected* becomes *true* for both the client and server sockets, and stays so until the connection is broken.

Given a communication domain, a protocol consists of a number of routines that together implement the services provided by a particular type of socket within the domain. Recall that *OSP* supports one domain (intramachine) having two protocols: the *PR_STREAM* protocol for stream sockets and the *PR_DGRAM* protocol for datagram sockets. The field *pr_sw* of *SOCKET* points to a *protocol switch*: a structure containing pointers to the procedures that constitute the protocol. Depending on the type of the socket, these routines will either be those of *PR_STREAM* or *PR_DGRAM*. Protocol switches are described more fully in the next subsection.

In the field *prrb*, every socket has a pointer to a *protocol request block*. This is used by the protocol layer to queue a request that cannot be granted immediately. (The definition of the prrb data type appears in Section 1.12, p. 67.) For example, a process issuing a send request on a stream socket will be suspended if the peer socket's buffer lacks sufficient space. This aspect of the socket layer is similar to resource management, module *RESOURCES*, and protocol request blocks are akin to resource request blocks. As explained later, processes may be suspended on send or receive requests to stream sockets, but only on receive requests to datagram sockets.

The field *num_msg* is used only by datagram sockets. It indicates the number of messages queued at the socket for reception. The field *dgram_msg_list* points to a queue of message descriptors that enables datagram sockets to distinguish individual messages within the input buffer, and thus preserve message boundaries. This is in contrast to stream sockets, where the flow of data is treated as a continuous stream of bytes and no structure is imposed on messages. The data type *DGRAM_BUF* is given by:

```
typedef struct dgram_buf_node DGRAM_BUF;
 struct dgram_buf_node    {
    char *so_name;              /* name of sending socket    */
    int num_bytes;              /* # of bytes in message     */
    DGRAM_BUF *next_msg;        /* next message              */
};
```

Note that, as for the field *so_inbuf* of *SOCKET*, only the size of a message is considered, and not its actual contents. The size of a message can range from 1 to *MAX_DATA* bytes, and hence the number of messages that can be queued at a datagram socket may vary. Since the size of the input buffer is limited to the constant *MAX_DATA*, the total of all the *num_bytes* fields in the queue cannot exceed *MAX_DATA*. Unlike stream sockets, in the datagram case, a send request that threatens to overflow the peer socket's buffer is discarded, since datagram sockets do not guarantee reliable communication. Note that *SIMCORE* will not generate a request to send a message of size more than *MAX_DATA*.

The *SO_ENTRY* structure is used to associate socket names (character strings) to sockets, and performs a function similar to that of the file directory (cf. *FILE_DIR_ENTRY* in module *FILES*). The name of a socket is given as a parameter when the socket is opened.

```
typedef struct so_entry_node SO_ENTRY;
struct so_entry_node    {
    char *so_name;              /* name bound to socket      */
    SOCKET *socket;             /* the corresponding socket  */
    SO_ENTRY *next;             /* list of socket entries    */
};
```

Socket entries are kept in the *socket directory* that, like the file directory, should provide efficient access to the socket structure, given a socket name. Each socket entry is associated with exactly one socket; i.e., a socket can be owned by exactly one process and cannot be shared. The process that creates the socket is its only owner. In some cases, a protocol may need to know the name of a socket given only a pointer to its socket structure. Module *SOCKETS* exports the routine *get_so_name*( ) for this purpose.

Other data type relevant to sockets are: *PCB* (p. 18), *PRRB* (p. 67), and *PRCB* (p. 66).

1.11.2 Socket-Protocol Interface

The field *pr_sw* of the *SOCKET* data type points to a *protocol switch*: a structure containing pointers to the procedures that constitute the protocol. Depending on the type of the socket, these routines will either be those of *PR_STREAM* or *PR_DGRAM*.

Although protocol switches introduce a level of indirection, they serve as a consistent interface to the protocol layer. This observation is most easily understood in the case of multiple communication domains. By going through the switch, socket layer routines can call a generic, with respect to the communication domain, protocol layer routine for a desired service. Given that the switch has been properly set when the sockets layer is first started up, the routine appropriate for the domain at hand will ultimately be called.

SIMCORE will pass pointers to the two switches when it calls *sockets_init*( ), which in turn must initialize the fields of the switch structures to point to the appropriate protocol layer procedures. (Procedure *sockets_init*( ) is explained more fully in Section 1.11.6.) Now, when a socket is opened, say of type stream, *open_sock*( ) sets the socket's *pr_sw* field to point to the stream protocol switch; for a datagram socket, the datagram protocol switch is used. The data type *PR_SW* is now defined:

```
typedef struct pr_sw_node PR_SW;
struct pr_sw_node   {
    int protocol_id;   /* 0 = PR_STREAM; 1 = PR_DGRAM */
    SO_TYPE so_type;   /* socket type: stream or dgram  */

/*       routines common to stream and datagram         */

    void (*pr_attach)( );
```

```
    void (*pr_detach)();
    union protocol_routines  {

/*              stream-specific routines                    */

        struct stream_only_routines   {
            EXIT_CODE (*pr_connect)();
            EXIT_CODE (*pr_disconnect)();
            void (*pr_accept)();
            void (*pr_send)();
            void (*pr_recv)();
            void (*pr_notify_recvd();
        } pr_stream;

/*              datagram-specific routines                  */

        struct dgram_only_routines   {
            EXIT_CODE (*pr_sendto)();
            void (*pr_recvfrom)();
        } pr_dgram;
    } pr_routines;
    int *hook;
};
```

The simulator creates uninitialized switch structures, one for stream sockets and one for datagram sockets, and provides *SOCKETS* with pointers to these structures by calling *sockets_init*( ); this routine is responsible for initializing these switches appropriately. For instance, they should be set so that *pr_sw→pr_routines.pr_stream.pr_send*( ) will point to the routine *stream_send*( )—see the table of *SOCKETS* external routines for the actual names of protocol routines to be used in switch structures.

Routines that are specific to either the stream protocol or the datagram protocol are kept in a union in the *PR_SW* structure. This reflects the fact that for a given socket, only stream routines or datagram routines, exclusively, will be called. To invoke a protocol routine, the socket layer simply calls the corresponding routine in the protocol switch pointed to by the field *pr_sw* of the socket structure. This, of course, will result in a one-level indirect call to the actual protocol routine. For example to invoke the protocol routine for sending to a stream socket, the socket layer would call *pr_sw→pr_routines.pr_stream.pr_send*( ). Observe that the socket does not need to know exactly which protocol is to be used. Everything has been taken care of at the time the protocol switch was initialized and when the *pr_sw* field of *SOCKET* was set. Of course, one could simply keep the pointers to the protocol routines *directly* in the socket structure, but this would lead to duplication of these pointers in each socket, thereby wasting memory and possibly leading to inconsistency problems when protocols are changed.

1.11.3 Calls Common to Stream and Datagram Sockets

We now describe in some detail the procedures implemented in the socket layer. A call to *open_sock*( ) opens and thereby creates a socket. The parameters are a pointer to a *SOCKET* structure (allocated by $\mathcal{SIMCORE}$), the socket type and the name to be given to the socket (a pointer to a string of characters). The following guidelines should be followed in writing the *open_sock*( ) procedure:

- Check the socket directory to see if a socket with this name already exists. If so return *fail*: unlike a file, a socket cannot be opened twice. Like module $\mathcal{FILES}$, where a table of open files is maintained, a table of open sockets should be maintained. The number of sockets that can be opened at any given time is limited to the constant *MAX_OPEN_SOCKETS*. If the table of open sockets is full then return *fail*; otherwise update the table of open sockets appropriately.
- Fill in the *SOCKET* template provided by $\mathcal{SIMCORE}$ as a parameter; i.e., initialize the fields *so_type*, *is_connected*, *is_accepting*, *so_inbuf*, *pcb*, *prrb*, and *so_error*. Also, the *pr_sw* pointer should be set to point to the appropriate protocol switch structure—see *sockets_init*( ).
- Create a new *SO_ENTRY* structure and fill in the socket name and the socket pointer. Add the new entry to the socket directory.
- Call the protocol routine *pr_attach*( ) and return *ok*. As described in Section 1.12, each protocol maintains a list of *protocol control blocks* (prcb), representing the sockets in need of the protocol's service. Procedure *pr_attach*( ) will allocate a prcb for the newly

created socket and add it to the protocol's prcb list.

A call to *close_sock*( ) discards a socket. For datagram sockets, which do not guarantee reliable communication, *close_sock*( ) first calls the protocol routine *pr_detach*( ) to allow the protocol to detach itself from the socket by deallocating the socket's prcb. If there is a pending request (prrb) for this socket, *pr_detach*( ) simply discards it along with the prcb. Upon returning from the protocol routine, the table of open sockets is updated and the socket's entry in the socket directory is deleted.

For stream sockets, the protocol routine *pr_disconnect*( ) is called to remove the connection between the socket and its peer. One of the parameters to *pr_disconnect*( ) is *purge_flag*, which should be set to *false*, indicating that the disconnection is due to a normal closing. The protocol should return *fail*, and consequently so should *close_sock*( ), if there is a request pending at the peer socket—stream sockets promise reliable delivery of data and the protocol must therefore refuse to close sockets that have not finished transmission. Otherwise, *pr_disconnect*( ) updates various data structures (the host prcb, the peer prcb, and the peer's socket structure) to reflect the disconnection, and returns *ok*. The socket may then be closed by updating its socket structure (*is_connected* gets *false*), calling *pr_detach*( ), and deleting its entry in the socket directory. Note that the peer socket structure is not updated at the socket layer—in real systems it may reside on another machine and it is up to the protocol layer to locate and update the peer socket.

Internal Routine (general socket calls)	**Called By**

EXIT_CODE open_sock `(so_type, socket, so_name);`
`SO_TYPE so_type;`
`SOCKET *socket;`
`char *so_name;`
Opens a new socket of type *so_type* and gives it the name *so_name*. Returns *fail* if a socket with *so_name* already exists.
	SIMCORE

EXIT_CODE close_sock `(socket);` `SOCKET *socket;` Closes an existing socket.	*SIMCORE*

1.11.4 Calls Specific to Stream Sockets

A call to *accept_sock*( ) marks a stream socket as ready to accept an incoming connection by setting the socket's *is_accepting* field to *true.* It then calls the protocol routine *pr_accept*( ); included in the call is a pointer *prrb* to a protocol request block, which *accept_sock*( ) obtained as a parameter from *SIMCORE*. Let *P* be the user process (simulated by *SIMCORE*) that called *accept_sock*( ). Then *pr_accept*( ) will suspend *P* on the event associated with the prrb until a connection request arrives.

A call to *connect_sock*( ) establishes a connection between two existing stream sockets. The actual connection is created by the protocol routine *pr_connect*( ). Procedure *connect_sock*( ) should return *fail* if the host socket is not of type *stream* or is already connected (since a stream socket can be connected to at most one peer socket), or if *pr_connect*( ) returns *fail.* Otherwise, *connect_sock*( ) marks the host socket as connected and returns *ok*. As when sockets are disconnected, the responsibility of updating the peer socket is delegated to the protocol layer.

A call to *send_sock*( ) results in the eventual transfer of data from the user's address space to the peer socket's input buffer. Besides the socket structure of the host socket, the parameters to *send_sock*( ) are *datalen*, the amount of data to be transferred (and not actual data), and *prrb*, a pointer to a protocol request block. The protocol routine *pr_send*( ) is called to perform the actual data transmission. Procedure *send_sock*( ) should return *fail* if the host socket is not of type *stream* or is not connected. If the peer socket's buffer lacks sufficient space to accommodate the message, then *pr_send*( ) suspends the sending process on the event associated with *prrb*.

A call to *recv_sock*( ) retrieves data from a socket's input buffer. Besides the socket structure, the parameters to *recv_sock*( ) are *datalen*, the amount of data to be received, and *prrb*, a pointer to a protocol request block. Since there is no real data exchange, *recv_sock*( ) simulates the receive action as follows: if at least *datalen* data resides in the buffer, then the field *so_inbuf* of the socket structure is updated appropriately, and the protocol routine *pr_notify_recvd*( ) is called. (By calling *pr_notify_recvd*( ), the protocol layer can decide if a previously suspended *send_sock*( ) request can now be accommodated.) Otherwise, the routine *pr_recv*( ) is called in order to suspend the receiving process on the event associated with *prrb*.

Internal Routine (stream socket calls)	**Called By**

EXIT_CODE connect_sock (socket, peer_so_name);
`SOCKET *socket;`
`char *peer_so_name;`
Makes a connection between two stream sockets.
	SIMCORE

EXIT_CODE accept_sock (socket, prrb);
`SOCKET *socket;`
`PRRB *prrb;`
Marks the stream socket as accepting a connection. The prrb pointer is delivered to the protocol layer via a call to *pr_accept*( ). The protocol layer will suspend the process on the prrb event until a connection request arrives. Returns *fail* if socket not of type stream or already connected.
	SIMCORE

EXIT_CODE send_sock (socket, datalen, prrb);
`SOCKET *socket;`
`int datalen;`
`PRRB *prrb;`
Sends data of length *datalen* to the peer stream socket. The parameter *prrb* is used by the protocol layer to suspend the process, if it has to.
	SIMCORE

EXIT_CODE recv_sock (socket, datalen, prrb);
`SOCKET *socket;`
`int datalen;`
`PRRB *prrb;`
Retrieves data from the stream socket's input buffer. In case of insufficient data, the protocol layer is called to suspend the process.
	SIMCORE

1.11.5 Calls Specific to Datagram Sockets

A call to *sendto_sock*( ) transmits data from one datagram socket to another. Since datagram transmission is connectionless, the name (character string) of the destination socket must be given explicitly as a parameter. Procedure *sendto_sock*( ) first checks if the socket type is *dgram* and then calls the protocol routine *pr_sendto*( ) to perform the

Internal Routine (datagram socket calls)	Called By

EXIT_CODE sendto_sock `(socket, peer_so_name, datalen);`
`SOCKET *socket;`
`char *peer_so_name;`
`int datalen;`
Sends data of length *datalen* to a datagram socket given by *peer_so_name*.
	SIMCORE

EXIT_CODE recvfrom_sock `(socket, datalen, prrb, sender);`
`SOCKET *socket;`
`int datalen;`
`PRRB *prrb;`
`char **sender;`
Retrieves data from a datagram socket's input buffer. *Sender* is a return parameter.
	SIMCORE

actual transfer. Unlike the stream case, the protocol layer is not provided with a prrb when *pr_sendto*( ) is called: if the request to send data to the destination datagram socket cannot be immediately satisfied, then it is simply discarded and *fail* is returned. In this case, *sendto_sock*( ) returns *fail* as well.

A call to *recvfrom_sock*( ) retrieves data from the input buffer of a datagram socket. Recall that datagram-based communication preserves message boundaries; i.e., a message obtained due to a single *recvfrom_sock*( ) call should correspond to a message transmitted due to a single *sendto_sock*( ) request. Message boundaries are preserved in module *SOCKETS* through the use of the list of datagram message descriptors (field *dgram_msg_list* of *SOCKET*) associated with every datagram socket. Each message in the list is kept in a *DGRAM_BUF* structure, which enables the socket layer to identify the name of the socket from which the message was transmitted.

Besides the socket structure, the parameters to *recvfrom_sock*( ) are *datalen*, the amount of data to be received; *prrb*, a pointer to a protocol request block; and *sender*, the address of a pointer to a string of characters representing the name of the socket whose message is ultimately consumed by the *recvfrom_sock*( ) call. *Sender* is a return parameter whose value is set when a message is chosen from the datagram socket's message list. It is up to the programmer to decide which message is returned to the process. For example, one could use a FIFO strategy, or select the first message that is big enough to satisfy the request. Whatever the strategy, if more data is present in the message than requested, the excess data is discarded. If less data is present than requested, then whatever is available is returned. Since no data is actually communicated in *OSP*, *recvfrom_sock*( ) simulates the receive action by updating the fields *so_inbuf* and *num_msg*, and deleting the selected message from the message list. If the socket's input buffer is empty (*socket*→*so_inbuf* = 0) at the time *recvfrom_sock*( ) is invoked, the protocol routine *pr_recvfrom* ( ) is called in order to suspend the receiving process on the event associated with *prrb*.

1.11.6 Miscellaneous Socket Calls

Procedure *sockets_init*( ) is called by *SIMCORE* once in order to initialize the protocol switch structures and any other data structure internal to *SOCKETS*. In particular, *SIMCORE* provides as parameters to *sockets_init*( ) two pointers to already existing but uninitialized protocol switch structures *PR_SW*. One switch structure should be initialized to point to the *PR_STREAM* protocol routines and the other to the *PR_DGRAM* protocol routines. Furthermore, the pointers to these switch structures should be saved. They will be needed whenever a new socket is opened to initialize the *pr_sw* field of the socket's *SOCKET* data structure. The choice of pointer for this field will, of course, depend upon the type of the socket.

Procedure *purge_sockets*( ), called by *PROCSVC* when a process terminates or is killed, removes any sockets left unclosed by the process. Upon finding such a socket in the table of open sockets, *purge_sockets*( ) executes a section of code that is similar to the code of *close_sock*( ) with one exception: it calls the protocol routine *pr_disconnect*( ) with *purge_flag* set to *true* when a stream socket is to be disconnected. Consequently, *pr_disconnect*( ) will disconnect the socket even if there is a request pending at the peer socket. Recall that under normal disconnection (*purge_flag* = *false*), *pr_disconnect*( ) will return *fail* if there is a pending request at the peer.

The last miscellaneous routine is *get_so_name*( ), which retrieves the name of a socket given only a pointer to this socket's data structure. This routine can be used by the *PROTOCOLS* module, which does not have direct access to the socket directory.

Internal Routine (miscellaneous calls)	Called By
sockets_init (stream_pr_sw, dgram_pr_sw); **PR_SW *stream_pr_sw, *dgram_pr_sw;** Called once by *SIMCORE* to allow for the initialization of the two protocol switch structures and any other internal data structures.	*SIMCORE*
purge_sockets (pcb); **PCB *pcb;** Purges the open sockets of process represented by *pcb*. Called by *PROCSVC* when a process terminates or is killed.	*PROCSVC*
char *get_so_name (socket); **SOCKET *socket;** Searches the socket directory and returns a pointer to the character string representing the name of the socket.	*PROTOCOLS*

External Routine	Host Module
extern stream_attach (/* socket */); **extern dgram_attach (/* socket */);** **/* SOCKET *socket; */** Called by *open_sock*( ) to inform the appropriate protocol that another socket requires its services. Protocol will allocate a prcb and append it to its prcb list.	*PROTOCOLS* *PROTOCOLS*
extern stream_detach (/* socket */); **extern dgram_detach (/* socket */);** **/* SOCKET *socket; */** Called by *close_sock*( ). Deallocates the prcb allocated to the socket.	*PROTOCOLS* *PROTOCOLS*
extern stream_accept (/* socket, prrb */); **/* SOCKET *socket;** **PRRB *prrb; */** Called by *accept_sock*( ) to suspend the process until a connection request arrives.	*PROTOCOLS*

External Routine (continued)	**Host Module**

extern stream_connect (/* socket, peer_name */);
`/* SOCKET *socket;`
`   char *peer_name;     */`
Called by *connect_sock*( ) to establish a connection between two stream sockets.
	PROTOCOLS

extern stream_disconnect (/* socket, purge_flag */);
`/* SOCKET *socket;`
`   BOOL purge_flag;     */`
Called by *close_sock*( ) and *purge_sockets*( ) to remove a connection. When called by *close_sock*( ), *purge_flag* will be *false* indicating that the disconnection is normal. In this case *stream_disconnect*( ) will return *fail* if there is a pending prrb. When called by *purge_sockets*( ), *purge_flag* will be *true* and *stream_disconnect*( ) will forcefully disconnect; a pending prrb will be discarded.
	PROTOCOLS

extern stream_send (/* socket, datalen, prrb */);
`/* SOCKET *socket;`
`   int datalen;`
`   PRRB *prrb;          */`
Called by *sock_send*( ) to perform actual transfer of data; will suspend process if peer socket's input buffer lacks sufficient space.
	PROTOCOLS

extern stream_recv (/* socket, datalen, prrb */);
`/* SOCKET *socket;`
`   int datalen;`
`   PRRB *prrb;          */`
Called by *recv_sock*( ) to suspend process when insufficient data in socket's input buffer.
	PROTOCOLS

extern stream_notify_recvd (/* socket */); `/* SOCKET *socket;      */` Called by *recv_sock*( ) after retrieving data from the input buffer of *socket*. Notifies the protocol layer that more space is available in the input buffer of this stream socket, so that a pending send request by this socket's peer can be initiated.	*PROTOCOLS*

<table>
<tr><th>External Routine (continued)</th><th>Host Module</th></tr>
<tr><td><pre>extern EXIT_CODE dgram_sendto(/*socket,
                         peer_name, datalen */);
   /* SOCKET *socket;
      char *peer_name;
      int datalen;   */</pre>Called by sendto_sock( ) to perform actual transfer; will discard message if receiving socket's buffer lacks space.</td><td>PROTOCOLS</td></tr>
<tr><td><pre>extern dgram_recvfrom (/* socket, datalen,
                                   prrb */);
   /* SOCKET *socket;
      int datalen;
      PRRB *prrb;   */</pre>Called by recvfrom_sock( ) when no data is present in the datagram socket's input buffer.</td><td>PROTOCOLS</td></tr>
</table>

1.12 Protocol-Level Support for Sockets – Module *PROTOCOLS*

OSP supports interprocess communication in the form of sockets, which are implemented in a layered fashion: user-level requests are directed to module *SOCKETS*, which relies on module *PROTOCOLS* to actually service the requests (see Figure 1.2, p. 50). *PROTOCOLS* exports two sets of procedures: those for protocol *PR_STREAM* and those for protocol *PR_DGRAM*. Protocol *PR_STREAM* achieves the reliable communication offered by stream sockets by enforcing end-to-end flow-control; i.e., suspending a sending process if the receiving socket's buffer is full. Protocol *PR_DGRAM* realizes datagram-based communication. To better understand the relationship between the socket and protocol layers, it is suggested that Section 1.11 be read before reading this section.

As described in Section 1.11, the protocol layer interacts with the socket layer via two protocol switch structures, one for stream sockets and one for datagram sockets. Each protocol switch contains pointers to the protocol routines needed to provide the services offered by the specific socket type. Although they introduce a level of indirection in accessing the protocol routines, protocol switches serve as a uniform interface to the protocol layer. For example, to establish a connection between two stream sockets, procedure *connect_sock*( ) of *SOCKETS* calls *pr_sw→pr_routines.pr_stream.pr_connect*( ), without knowing which protocol will actually be used. This call results in the invocation of procedure *stream_connect*( ) of *PROTOCOLS*. Moreover, *connect_sock*( ) would issue exactly the same call if another protocol were substituted for the one currently supported by *OSP* .

The data types employed by *PROTOCOLS* are now given. The first two are not predefined in *OSP* but their use should facilitate the implementation of the protocol layer.

```
typedef struct pr_entry_node PR_ENTRY;
struct pr_entry_node {
    int protocol_id;  /* 0 = PR_STREAM, 1 = PR_DGRAM;  */
                      /* set by programmer             */
    PRCB *prcb;       /* list of protocol control blocks */
    int *hook;
};
```

A protocol entry structure can be used to represent each protocol implemented in the protocol layer. The procedure *protocols_init*( ) should allocate and initialize these structures when called by the simulator. The field *prcb* points to a list of protocol control blocks, which represents the sockets currently using this protocol, and their connections, if any.

```
typedef struct prcb_node PRCB;
struct prcb_node {
    char *host_so_name;  /* name of host socket          */
    SOCKET *host_socket; /* socket using this protocol   */
    SOCKET *peer_socket; /* peer connected to this host  */
    PRCB *next;          /* optional next prcb           */
    PRCB *prev;          /* optional prev prcb           */
};
```

Protocol control blocks are allocated and initialized by *stream_attach*( ) and *dgram_attach*( ). These routines are called by the socket layer to inform the protocol of the existence of a new socket.

Fields of type *SOCKET* refer to socket structures, the main data structure of the socket layer (p. 52). For stream sockets, the field *peer_socket* is set by *stream_connect*( ). Datagram-based communication is connectionless. When a datagram send/receive request is received by the protocol layer it is accompanied by the name of the peer socket; the *host_so_name* fields of the prcb list of the datagram protocol entry can then be examined to locate the peer socket. Finally, prcb's are deleted by *stream_detach*( ) and *dgram_detach*( ).

Protocol control blocks play an important role in distributed systems. They provide access to the socket structures of peer processes that may be located anywhere within the network. Even though *OSP* supports only intramachine communication, it is still designed so that peer sockets are inaccessible at the socket layer, and accessible at the protocol layer only through prcb's.

The protocol request block (prrb) data type is predefined in *OSP* as follows:

```
typedef struct prrb_node PRRB;
struct prrb_node {
    int prrb_id;            /* used by trace facility,        */
                            /* set by simulator               */
    int protocol_id;        /* 0=PR_STREAM, 1=PR_DGRAM        */
    SOCKET *socket;         /* socket involved in request     */
    SO_ACTION so_action;    /* requested action               */
    int msglen;             /* msg length to be transmitted   */
    EVENT *event;           /* event for waitsvc and sigsvc   */
    PCB *pcb;               /* process that issued request    */
    int *hook;
};
```

The protocol layer assembles a prrb each time a socket layer request cannot be immediately satisfied. For example, a send request must be put on hold if the input buffer of the peer socket lacks sufficient space to accommodate the message. In order to safeguard against errant pointers, all prrb's, and their associated event structures, are allocated by the simulator. They are then passed to the socket layer via simulator-generated calls to socket routines, and ultimately to the protocol layer via socket layer calls to protocol routines.

1.12.1 Stream Protocol Calls

We now describe in some detail the procedures exported by the protocol layer.

Procedure *stream_attach*( ) is called by the socket layer when a stream socket is created. A prcb is allocated for the new socket, initialized appropriately, and then appended to the prcb list of the stream protocol entry structure.

Procedure *stream_detach*( ) is called when a stream socket is closed. The prcb allocated to this socket is removed from the prcb list of the stream entry structure and then deallocated.

Procedure *stream_accept*( ) is called by *accept_sock*( ). A prrb, provided in template form by the simulator via the socket layer, is assembled. The event field of the prrb is used to suspend the calling process until a connection request arrives. (Process control monitor calls are explained in Section 1.5.2.)

Procedure *stream_connect*( ), called by *connect_sock*( ), establishes a connection between two stream sockets. The parameters to *stream_connect*( ) are the host socket structure and the name of the peer socket to which the connection should be made. The exit code *fail* is returned if the peer socket cannot be found in the prcb list of the stream socket entry, if the peer is not accepting connections, or if the peer is already connected. Otherwise a connection is established by updating the host and peer prcb's, the peer socket structure, signaling the peer process using the event in the peer socket's prrb, and returning *ok*. The host socket structure is modified at the socket layer upon return from this routine.

Procedure *stream_disconnect*( ) removes a connection. The parameters to *stream_disconnect*( ) are the host socket structure and the variable *purge_flag*. A value of *false* for *purge_flag* indicates that the disconnection is normal, i.e., due to socket layer routine *close_sock*( ). In this case, if there is a request pending at the host socket, *stream_disconnect*( ) should return *fail*—stream sockets promise reliable delivery of data and the protocol must therefore refuse to close sockets that have not finished transmission. Otherwise, the connection is removed by updating the host and peer prcb's, the peer socket structure, and returning *ok*.

A value of *true* for *purge_flag* means that the disconnection is due to the termination of the process that owns the host socket. In this case, disconnection proceeds as above, even if there is a request pending at the host socket. The peer process associated with the prrb is awakened by the prrb event, and the field *so_error* of the peer socket is set to *true.* This will convey to the peer process that the process to which it was connected has terminated.

Procedure *stream_send*( ) is called by *send_sock*( ) to send data to a connected socket. The parameters to *stream_send*( ) are the host socket, the length of the data to be transmitted, and a prrb to be used to suspend the calling process if the send request cannot be immediately satisfied. This procedure first locates the peer socket via the host's prcb. The following scenarios are then possible:

1. The input buffer of the peer socket has sufficient space to accommodate the data transfer, and no receive request is pending at the peer socket. Then *stream_send*( ) performs the transfer simply by updating the integer field *so_inbuf* of the peer socket—as described in Section 1.11, flow of data is simulated in $\mathcal{OSP}$ by keeping track of the amount of data in a socket's input buffer; the data content is left unspecified.

2. The peer socket cannot accommodate the data and no receive request is pending at the peer socket. In this case, *stream_send*( ) will transfer as much data into the peer socket's input buffer as space permits—once again by updating the peer socket's *so_inbuf* field. Procedure *stream_send*( ) then assembles its prrb parameter requesting transfer of the remaining data, attaches the prrb to the host socket structure, and uses the prrb event to suspend the process that issued the send request.

3. The peer socket can accommodate the data and a receive request is pending at the peer socket. Then *stream_send*( ) performs the transfer by updating the peer socket's *so_inbuf* field. If this input buffer now contains sufficient data to satisfy the pending request, the *so_inbuf* field of the peer socket is updated once again, this time to reflect the receive action; the peer socket's prrb field is set to NULL, and the process suspended on the request is awakened by signaling the event in the peer socket's prrb. Otherwise, i.e., when the pending receive request can still not be satisfied, *stream_send*( ) just returns.

4. The peer socket cannot accommodate the data and a receive request is pending at the peer socket. Then, as described in case (**2**),

stream_send( ) transfers as much data as possible into the input buffer of the peer socket, and suspends the sending process on a request to transfer the remaining data. The input buffer of the peer socket will now be full, and *stream_send*( ) can safely signal the process awaiting the arrival of data at the peer socket.

Procedure *stream_recv*( ) is called by *recv_sock*( ) if there is not enough data in a socket's input buffer to satisfy a receive request. The parameters to *stream_recv*( ) are the host socket, the length of data to be received, and a prrb allocated by the simulator. This procedure assembles the prrb, attaches it to the host socket, and suspends the process that issued the call to *recv_sock*( ) on the event contained in the prrb.

Procedure *stream_notify_recvd*( ) is called by *recv_sock*( ) of the socket layer to inform the protocol layer that more space is available in a socket's input buffer. It first checks if a send request is pending at the peer socket. If not, *stream_notify_recvd*( ) simply returns. Otherwise, it initiates a transfer of data into the host socket's input buffer. If there is enough space to fully accommodate the request, then *stream_notify_recvd*( ) updates the *so_inbuf* field of the host socket, sets the prrb field of the peer socket to NULL, and signals the process suspended on the event contained in the peer socket's prrb. If the message

Internal Routine (stream protocol calls)	**Called By**
stream_attach `(socket);` `SOCKET *socket;` Called by *open_sock*( ); allocates a prcb for the socket and adds it to the protocol's prcb list.	*SOCKETS*
stream_detach `(socket);` `SOCKET *socket;` Called by *close_sock*( ) and *purge_sockets*( ); detaches the socket from the protocol by removing the socket's prcb from the protocol's prcb list.	*SOCKETS*

stream_accept `(socket, prrb);`
`SOCKET *socket;`
`PRRB *prrb;`
Called by *accept_sock*( ) to suspend process until a connection request arrives.
	SOCKETS

can only be partially accommodated, then *stream_notify_recvd*( ) sets the *so_inbuf* field of the host socket to *MAX_DATA*, and decrements the *msglen* field of the peer socket's prrb accordingly.

Internal Routine (stream calls, continued)	**Called By**
EXIT_CODE stream_connect `(socket, peer_so_name);` `SOCKET *socket;` `char *peer_so_name;` Called by *connect_sock*( ) to establish connection between two stream sockets.	*SOCKETS*
EXIT_CODE stream_disconnect `(socket, purge_flag);` `SOCKET *socket;` `BOOL purge_flag;` Called by *close_sock*( ), with *purge_flag* set to *false*, to remove a connection between two stream sockets. Returns *fail* if there is a pending prrb at the peer socket. Also called by *purge_sockets*( ), with *purge_flag* set to *true*; disconnects even if there is pending prrb, which is discarded.	*SOCKETS*
stream_send `(socket, datalen, prrb);` `SOCKET *socket;` `int datalen;` `PRRB *prrb;` Called by *send_sock*( ) to send data from one stream socket to another. Blocks sending process, if receiving socket lacks sufficient space. Wakes up process at the receiving socket if it had been suspended on a receive request.	*SOCKETS*
stream_recv `(socket, datalen, prrb);` `SOCKET *socket;` `int datalen;` `PRRB *prrb;` Called by *recv_sock*( ) if not enough data in the socket's buffer; will block process till requested amount of data arrives.	*SOCKETS*

Internal Routine (stream calls, continued)	**Called By**
stream_notify_recvd `(socket);` `SOCKET *socket;` Called by *recv_sock*( ) to initiate possible pending send request; may wake up peer process if send request is serviced entirely.	*SOCKETS*

1.12.2 Datagram Protocol Calls

Procedure *dgram_attach*( ) is called by the socket layer when a datagram socket is created. A prcb is allocated for the new socket, initialized appropriately, and then appended to the prcb list of the datagram protocol entry structure.

Procedure *dgram_detach*( ) is called when a datagram socket is closed. The prcb allocated to this socket is removed from the prcb list of the datagram entry structure and then deallocated.

Procedure *dgram_sendto*( ) is called by *sendto_sock*( ) of the socket layer to send data from one datagram socket to another. The parameters to *dgram_sendto*( ) are the host socket, the length of the message to be sent, and the name of the peer socket. The exit code *fail* is returned if the peer socket cannot be found in the prcb list of the datagram socket entry, or if the peer socket is not of type *dgram*. Otherwise, the following scenarios are possible:

1. There is enough space in the peer socket's input buffer to accommodate the message, and no receive request is pending at the peer socket. Then *dgram_sendto*( ) appends a new message descriptor to the peer socket's field *dgram_msg_list* (p. 1.11.1), and updates the peer socket's *so_inbuf* and *num_msg* fields.

2. There is enough space in the peer socket's input buffer to accommodate the message, and a receive request is pending at the peer socket. Then *dgram_sendto*( ) only needs to set the prrb field of the peer socket to NULL and wake up the process suspended on the receive request by signaling the event in the peer socket's prrb. This amounts to the suspended process receiving the just-arrived message. Note that the length of the message received may not be the same as the length requested, but exactly one message is received; i.e., message boundaries are preserved as required of datagram-

based communication.

3. The peer socket cannot accommodate the message. Then *dgram_sendto*( ) simply discards the message by returning without any further action. (Remember that datagram-based communication is not reliable.)

Procedure *dgram_recv*( ) is called by *recvfrom_sock*( ) of the socket layer when no message is present in the host socket's input buffer. This procedure assembles its prrb parameter, attaches it to the host socket structure, and suspends the calling process on the event contained in the prrb.

Internal Routine (datagram protocol calls)	**Called By**
dgram_attach (socket); `SOCKET *socket;` Called by *open_sock*( ); allocates a prcb for the socket and adds it to the datagram protocol's prcb list.	*SOCKETS*
dgram_detach (socket); `SOCKET *socket;` Called by *close_sock*( ) and *purge_sockets*( ); detaches the socket from the datagram protocol by removing the socket's prcb from the protocol's prcb list.	*SOCKETS*

EXIT_CODE dgram_sendto (socket, peer_so_name, datalen);
`SOCKET *socket;`
`char *peer_so_name;`
`int datalen;`
Called by *sendto_sock*( ) to send data from one datagram socket to another; will discard message if receiving socket lacks sufficient buffer space.
	SOCKETS

dgram_recvfrom (socket, datalen, prrb);
`SOCKET *socket;`
`int datalen;`
`PRRB *prrb;`
Called by *recvfrom_sock*( ) to suspend process on a receive request.
	SOCKETS

Internal Routine (miscellaneous calls)	Called By
void protocols_init ( ); Called by the simulator to allow for the initialization of protocol entry structures and other internal data structures.	*SIMCORE*

External Routine	Host Module
extern gen_int_handler ( ); Called to wake up or suspend processes.	*INTER*
extern char *get_so_name (`/* socket */`); `/* SOCKET *socket; */` Searches the socket directory and returns pointer to the character string representing the name of the socket.	*SOCKETS*

2

USING *OSP*

2.1 Getting Started

Welcome to the *OSP* user's guide. Over the course of the semester, your instructor will assign a series of projects in which one or more modules of *OSP* are to be implemented. *OSP* assumes that for each assignment a separate directory is installed in the class account. Throughout this chapter we will be using ~**OS_class_acnt** as the name of the class account, and **assign.xyz** as the name of the directory for a given assignment.

Working under UNIX, it is a good idea to take steps toward protecting your files from unauthorized copying. The most convenient way to do this is by putting the command

```
umask 077
```

in the **.login** file in your home directory. Then type "`source ~/.login`". This will ensure that the files and directories you create will not have read or write permission for anyone other than yourself. If you have already created files or directories prior to performing this procedure, you can still protect them by typing "`chmod 700 filename`" for each file you wish to protect.

Before starting to implement a module of *OSP*, copy the following files from the assignment directory ~**OS_class_acnt/assign.xyz**:

1. The **Makefile** – contains all the instructions for compiling your modules and linking them to *OSP*;

2. For each module $\mathcal{M}$ that you are asked to implement, the **M.c** file;
3. The source file **dialog.c** – contains routines you can use for debugging (see Section 1.4).

The **M.c** files contain skeletons of the modules (in C format) to be implemented. A module skeleton consists of declarations of all standard *OSP* data structures needed by the module, and headings of all exported routines, i.e., routines called by other modules. Module skeletons ensure a consistent interface to *OSP*: you need only fill in the empty bodies of the exported routines. You may create your own internal data structures and write your own internal routines, but you *should not* change any declarations originally given to you in the skeleton.

2.2 Compiling *OSP*

Student-implemented modules are compiled and linked to *OSP* as follows:

1. Make sure that the **M.c** file are in the same directory as the Makefile.
2. Type the UNIX command "`make`".

If your modules are syntactically correct, and the above guidelines have been observed, the **M.o** files for each module and the executable file, called **OSP**, will be created in the same directory as Makefile.

2.3 Running *OSP*

To run the simulator, just type "`OSP`". When the simulator starts, it will prompt you for the *simulation parameters*. The simulator uses these parameters to decide whether the system should be I/O-bound or cpu-bound, how often there should be a memory, I/O, or resource request, how long the simulation should run, etc. The instructor will probably specify the parameters that are expected in the final run(s), but for debugging purposes you can choose your own. Simulation pa-

parameter	valid range	suggested range
process creation intensity	1 to 10	4 to 10
avg cpu time per process	20 and up	60 to 500
overall event frequency	1 to 10	4 to 10
share of memory events	$1 \leq m \leq 10 - i - r - s$	same
share of I/O events	$1 \leq i \leq 10 - m - r - s$	same
share of resource events	$1 \leq r \leq 10 - m - i - s$	same
share of sockets events	$1 \leq s \leq 10 - m - i - r$	same
sockets simulation mode	*s*(tream) / *d*(gram) / *b*(oth)	same
cpu time quantum	5 to $4 \cdot \alpha$	$\alpha/5$ to α
degree of prepaging	0 to 10	0 to 4
memory reference pattern	*l*(ocal) / *r*(andom)	same
deadlock detect/avoid	*d* / *a*	same
simulation time	2,000 and up	20,000 to 100,000
number of snapshots	1 to 30	2 to 10
trace switch	1 (on)/ 0 (off)	same
interactive run	*y* / *n*	same

TABLE 2.1 *OSP* Simulation Parameters: m, i, r, s denote shares of memory, I/O, resource, and socket events, respectively; α denotes the average cpu time per process.

rameters specified at the beginning of a run are saved in the file **simulation.parameters** in your working directory, and by renaming this file you can create archives of different sets of simulation parameters. To run *OSP* with the parameters saved in an archives file, simply type

```
OSP a_parameter_file
```

Table 2.1 describes the simulation parameters used by *OSP*.

Most of the parameters are self-explanatory. The intensity of process creation determines the average number of active processes at any given time during simulation. Intensity 1 corresponds to about 1.5 active processes on the average, while intensity 10 corresponds to about 15 processes. When the current number of active processes significantly deviates from the intended number, the simulator speeds up or slows down its process creation activity accordingly. Average cpu time per process is the average amount of time a process will use the cpu. The overall event intensity indicates the rate at which I/O, resource, and memory requests will be generated in the system. The total number of requests is then divided in accordance with the three parameters indicating the share of each type of request. The memory referencing pattern generated by *OSP* may be either random or local. The latter realizes the "locality principle" where the referencing of memory by processes drifts slowly from page to page without many sudden jumps. The *l/r* option enables comparative testing of such memory management strategies as prepaging, working set model, and others.

Once the parameters have been entered, module *SIMCORE* will begin generating events that simulate the execution of user programs. In addition, *SIMCORE* simulates the interrupts of the timer and I/O devices. The particular types of events generated are:

- requests for process creation, termination, and abortion
- requests for suspending and awakening processes
- requests to send and receive messages over sockets
- I/O requests
- requests for resources
- references to virtual memory
- timer interrupts
- device interrupts

During simulation, you may view periodically the system status, e.g., the state of memory and devices, various statistics accumulated by the simulator, etc. The simulation parameter *snapshot_interval* indicates how often during simulation the system status is to be displayed. A snapshot can also be requested by hitting CTRL-Z. Each snapshot break also presents an opportunity to interactively change the simulation parameters, and, perhaps, variables local to modules you have implemented (also see Section 1.4).

The interactive run parameter, if set to "no", prohibits the run-time change of simulation parameters at snapshots, and simulation will proceed without interruption. This can save you time when interaction with *OSP* is not needed. In the noninteractive mode, the output generated by the simulator and your program is saved in the file **simulation.run**. If this file already exists, it will be overwritten. However, if *OSP* is run with the "*-a*" option (*OSP -a*), the new run will be appended to the old one(s). In interactive mode, the output is directed to the screen and is not saved in a file. However, you can always use the UNIX script facility to record the terminal session.

Normally, the events generated by *OSP* will be different from run to run, since the simulator is driven by a random number generator. Sometimes it may be useful to repeat the previous sequence of events generated by the simulator, for example, to compare different versions of the same module or to reproduce an error message exactly as it occurred in the previous run. The "*-d*" option (for debugging) can be used for this purpose. First run *OSP* per normal, entering the simulation parameters interactively. As described above, the simulation parameters are saved in the file **simulation.parameters**; what we didn't mention is that the *seed* used by the random number generator is also saved in this file. To direct the simulator to reuse this seed on the next run, and thus reproduce the sequence of events generated in the previous run, type[1]

```
OSP -d simulation.parameters
```

Since in the non-interactive mode the standard output is redirected into a file, you cannot use *stdout* to print messages on the screen. If this becomes necessary—for example, to generate a prompt for input that will direct module *MEMORY* to switch from one memory management algorithm to another—another file attached to the device **/dev/tty** should be opened. Messages printed on this file are not redirected and will appear on the screen. For example,

```
terminal_fp = fopen("/dev/tty","w");
fprintf(terminal\_fp, "\nHello... Want something? ");
scanf("%s", answer);
fclose(terminal_fp);
```

will print a message to the terminal and then read from the standard input.

[1]If *OSP* is run on a parameter file, say **my.parameters**, the seed is saved in that file. The events of the previous run can then be reproduced by running "`OSP -d my.parameters`".

2.4 Interpreting the Statistics

The simulator accumulates statistics that reflect the amount of resources consumed by the various modules. They can be used to estimate the performance of your modules. Moreover, if you find that the statistics being reported deviate largely from those produced by **OSP.demo**, then a bug may be lurking in your implementation. Most significant are the following indicators:

- system throughput
- average waiting time per process
- average turnaround time per process
- cpu utilization
- memory utilization

Superior performance is reflected in lower system throughput, average waiting time, and average turnaround time; and in higher cpu and memory utilization. Note that the average turnaround time of processes is generally a better indication of system performance than the system throughput. This is because the latter is more susceptible to such arbitrary factors as the number of processes left in the waiting and ready queues at the end of simulation.

OSP also generates a number of auxiliary statistics:

- total number of tracks swept on each device
- average number of tracks swept per I/O request
- average turnaround time per read/write request
- total number of pages swapped in
- total number of pages swapped out

These statistics reflect the quality of the device management and page replacement and allocation strategies. The lower these numbers are, the better. In fact, these latter statistics are usually more indicative about the quality of device schedulers and memory managers than system throughput and other parameters in the first category. The output of the simulator also contains information about the number of locked and dirty frames, the status of the frame and device table, the average number of active processes during simulation, etc. Like the statistics, this information is useful for gauging performance and debugging.

Statistics generated by **OSP.demo** can also be used for demonstrating material presented in class. For example, by altering the length of the cpu time quantum, one can see its effect on the overall system throughput, average process turnaround time, and other statistics.

Likewise, by varying the degree of prepaging the student can observe the effect of prepaging on the number of page faults, on the total number of pages swapped in or out, and on the average turnaround time. For instance, an increase in the prepaging degree will noticeably reduce the number of pages swapped in due to page faults, However, prepaging will increase the number of pages swapped in each time a process is dispatched for execution. Because of this tradeoff, the overall number of pages swapped in or out should decrease until an optimal degree of prepaging is reached (usually 2 to 4). At this point, the number of swapped pages will start to go up. The optimal degree of prepaging depends on how good the prepaging algorithm is at guessing which pages might be needed in the future. The effectiveness of prepaging may depend on other factors as well. For example, if the time quantum is short or if interrupts are frequent, processes may not be able to enjoy benefits of prepaging. (Why?)

In order to better understand the behavior of the LRU page replacement algorithm, you can run **OSP.demo** with randomized and localized memory referencing patterns. The number of page replacements will be less under the localized pattern. The intensity of memory references should be set sufficiently high (e.g., at least 2) to ensure that the random fluctuations do not obscure this effect.

Similarly, it can be demonstrated that usually the average turnaround time per read/write request increases with the intensity of I/O requests. There may be some exceptions though. For instance, if the disk scheduling algorithm is very good at scheduling closely grouped requests, then the average turnaround time may actually decrease. However, this trend is temporary, and an even higher I/O intensity will cause the turnaround time to increase.

For resource handling, the average process turnaround time and the system throughput are the main parameters to watch. However, for deadlock avoidance, the size of the waiting queue is also an interesting parameter. For deadlock detection, a parameter of interest is the number of processes killed, since it indicates the quality of the deadlock resolution algorithm.

Sometimes changing simulation parameters and algorithms may have unexpected effect on the statistics generated by *OSP*. This is partly due to the fact that, as in any complex system, different factors may work in opposite directions. For instance, under a high intensity of resource requests, better cpu scheduling will give *SIMCORE* an opportunity to generate more such requests. This may result in a higher number of suspended processes than would be the case under a less successful cpu scheduling strategy. Likewise, poorly conceived cpu scheduling, device scheduling, or resource handling strategies may slow down the processing. One might expect that under these circumstances the number of active processes should begin to grow. However, this won't happen on a grand scale, since the simulator will try to avoid flooding the system with a large number of processes. On the other hand, the throughput *will* be lower and the turnaround time *will* be greater, as expected.

2.5 Submitting Assignments

As before, we assume that **~OS_class_acnt/assign.xyz** is the directory for the current assignment. The instructor will place several files of simulation parameters in this directory, such as

```
run.with.trace
run.high.event.intensity
```

and will ask you to use these parameter files for the final run. You may also submit simulation runs with your own parameters, if requested by the instructor. The routine **hand_in** in the assignment directory automates this process. To submit your runs make sure that:

1. The source code of your modules is in the current working directory.

2. Your program compiles correctly with the *original* Makefile that you copied from the assignment account.[2]

3. The parameter files to be used for the final runs are readable. Do *not* attempt to create parameter files by any means other than by running *OSP*; if a parameter file is incorrect, *OSP* may suspend itself, and the output will not be produced.

4. The "interactive run" parameter is set to '*n*'.

Next, type:

```
~OS_class_acnt/assign.xyz/hand_in
```

The **hand_in** program asks for the names of the students that have worked jointly on the assignment, and informs them if and when they have submitted this assignment before. Don't worry—**hand_in** will always ask for authorization to override a previous submission. Then it compiles your modules and links them to the rest of *OSP*. After compilation, it asks which parameter files to use (expecting just the top-level names, not full path names) and executes the program with each of the parameter sets specified. The top-level name of any student-supplied parameter file should be different from any of the top-level names of parameter files in the assignment directory of the class account. This is because, **hand_in** first searches the assignment directory for parameter files; if unsuccessful, only then will it search the student's current working directory.

Before each run, you are given a chance to insert comments in the output, if you or the instructor so desire. These comments will conveniently appear just before the output generated by the run. The **hand-in** program places a file consisting of the sources of your modules, the output of compilation, and the output of the simulation runs, into an unreadable file in a subdirectory of the class account. A copy of the output (excluding the sources) can also be found in the **simulation.run** file of your working directory.

An assignment can be submitted more than once, but only the last version will be saved in the class account. However, since the submission time and date are recorded in each version submitted, an assignment cannot be submitted after the deadline without the permission of the

[2] The original Makefile may be modified to suit one's particular needs during the debugging phase. However, the **hand_in** program *requires* that the original Makefile be used.

instructor.

It is important to keep in mind that **hand_in** executes *OSP* in non-interactive mode, so the messages printed on **stdout** will not appear on the screen. As explained earlier, you can open a file on **/dev/tty** to view such messages.

2.6 Errors and Warnings

In order to prevent corruption to the integrity of the system state, the simulator maintains its own internal copy which cannot be accessed by the other modules. Whenever an inconsistency is detected by the simulator, it terminates with an informative error message or issues a warning and continues. For example, a reference to virtual memory that should cause a page fault but doesn't, will result in the simulator terminating with an error, while if the "dirty bit" optimization is not used in memory management, a warning is issued. All error and warning messages are self-explanatory.

OSP has rather sophisticated error-checking capabilities and, therefore, if no error is reported during a simulation run, it is a strong indication that your program is correct. Since, however, *OSP* simulation is driven by a random sequence of events, errors can occur in one run but not in another. Therefore, to verify correctness of your *OSP* implementation, you should run it on several different sets of simulation parameters.

Sometimes you may get a *segmentation fault*, one of the difficult-to-detect programming errors. In a large modular system like *OSP*, segmentation faults are even harder to pinpoint, especially when the debugger points in the direction of one of the modules you did not write. However, there is only a slim chance that an *OSP* module is to blame. Usually the segmentation fault is a result of a bad parameter passed to the external routines of the module you are implementing. The segmentation fault may also be caused by a modification to a data structure in the header of a template file module.c. This should not be done under any circumstances. One final advice: using **lint**, the C type checker, may help spot problems at an early stage.

GLOSSARY

BOOL – the boolean data type, 6

DEADLOCK_TYPE – enumeration type for deadlock handling methods, 46

DEV_ENTRY – the device entry data type, 34

DGRAM_BUF – datagram buffers type, 54

Deadlock_Method – global variable determining deadlock handling method, 46

Dev_Tbl – the device table data structure, 34

EVENT – data type for events, 18

EXIT_CODE – exit codes used by *OSP* routines, 6

FILE_DIR_ENTRY – data type for an entry in file directory, 38

FRAME – the frame data type, 6

Frame_Tbl – the frame table, 6

INODE – the UNIX-style i-node data type, 39

INT_TYPE – the type of interrupts, 5

INT_VECTOR – the interrupt vector data type, 5

IORB – the input/output request block data type, 34

IO_ACTION – the type of input/output requests, 6

Int_Vector – the interrupt vector, 5

MAX_BLOCK – the number of blocks on a device, 33

MAX_DATA – size of the socket buffer, 53

MAX_DEV – size of the device table, 34

MAX_FRAME – size of the physical memory, 6

MAX_PAGE – the maximum size of page tables, 24

MAX_PCB – maximum number of active pcb's at any given time, 44

MAX_RSRC – maximum number of resources in system resource table, 46

MAX_TRACK – the number of tracks on a device, 33

OFILE – data type for entries in the open file table, 39

PAGE_ENTRY – the page entry data type, 23

PAGE_SIZE – the size of a page in bytes, 5

PAGE_TBL – the page table data type, 24

PCB – the process control block data type, 18

PRCB – the protocol control block data type, 66

PRRB – the protocol request block data type, 67

PR_ENTRY – the protocol entry data type, 66

PR_SW – the protocol switch structure, 55

PTBR – the page table base register, 6

Prepage_Degree – global variable regulating degree of prepaging, 24

Quantum – global variable holding the time quantum, 31

REFER_ACTION – the type of memory references, 7

RESOURCE – data type for resource entries in resource table, 46

RRB – the resource request block data type, 46

Resource_Tbl – the resource table, 46

SOCKET – the socket data type, 52

SO_ACTION – the type of socket actions, 52

SO_ENTRY – the socket entry data type, 54

SO_TYPE – socket types, 52

STATUS – process status type, 18

TRACK_SIZE – the track size on each of the devices, 33